21.40

D0341684

=== *Dynamic Modern Women* ===

CHAMPIONS

OF

EQUALITY

Laurie Lindop

Twenty-First Century Books
A Division of Henry Holt and Company
New York

For Ellen Abdow, for everything

≈

Twenty-First Century Books
A Division of Henry Holt and Company, Inc.
115 West 18th Street
New York, NY 10011

Henry Holt® and colophon are trademarks of
Henry Holt and Company, Inc.
Publishers since 1866

Published in Canada by Fitzhenry & Whiteside Ltd.
195 Allstate Parkway, Markham, Ontario, L3R 4T8

Library of Congress Cataloging-in-Publication Data
Lindop, Laurie.
Champions of equality / by Laurie Lindop.
p. cm.—(Dynamic modern women)
Includes bibliographical references and index.
Summary: Biographies of the following women who have made contributions
toward furthering equality: Margarethe Cammermeyer, Marian Wright Edelman,
Myrlie Evers-Williams, Elizabeth Glaser, Delores Huerta, Patricia Ireland,
Maggie Kuhn, Wilma Mankiller, Vilma Martinez, and Eleanor Holmes Norton.
1. Women—United States—Biography—Juvenile literature. 2. Women
social reformers—United States—Biography—Juvenile literature.
3. Civil rights—United States—Juvenile literature. 4. Equality—United
States—Juvenile literature. [1. Social reformers. 2. Civil rights workers.
3. Women—Social conditions. 4. Women—Biography.] I. Title.
II. Series: Lindop, Laurie. Dynamic modern women.
HQ1412.L562 1997
303.48'4'092273—dc21
[B]   96-39557
                                                                CIP
                                                                AC

ISBN 0-8050-4165-6
First Edition—1997

Designed by Kelly Soong

Printed in Mexico
All first editions are printed on acid-free paper.∞
1 3 5 7 9 10 8 6 4 2

Photo credits

p. 6: ©Barry King/Gamma Liaison; p. 18: ©T. Westenberger/Gamma Liaison; p. 30: ©Cynthia Johnson/Gamma Liaison; p. 40: ©Michael Grecco/Sygma; pp. 52, 76. ©AP/Wide World Photos; p. 64:©Wally McNamee/Sygma; p. 86: ©James Schnepf/Gamma Liaison; p. 96: ©Tony Korody/Sygma; p. 106: ©Rick Reinhard/Impact Visuals.

CONTENTS

Introduction   5

One   Margarethe Cammermeyer   7

Two   Marian Wright Edelman   19

Three   Myrlie Evers-Williams   31

Four   Elizabeth Glaser   41

Five   Delores Huerta   51

Six   Patricia Ireland   61

Seven   Maggie Kuhn   73

Eight   Wilma Mankiller   83

Nine   Vilma Martinez   93

Ten   Eleanor Holmes Norton   103

Source Notes   111

Further Reading   121

Index   123

INTRODUCTION

The United States was established on the principle that "all men are created equal." Originally the Founding Fathers envisioned this to mean that all white men are created equal. The women you will read about in this book have fought to ensure that this basic ideal of equality is expanded so that it applies to all citizens.

Many have encountered discrimination in their own lives. They have been barred from attending certain schools because of the color of their skin. They have been told that they will not succeed because of their ethnicity or because they are female. They have witnessed firsthand how prejudice is fueled when some people wish to hold others down in order that they might rise. All of the women have realized that such discrimination is not the promise nor the hope of America, and they have dedicated their lives to making certain that all citizens are treated equally under the law. Through their work they have brought greater opportunities to more people and have made our nation more just. They are true Champions of Equality

ONE

❦

MARGARETHE CAMMERMEYER

For twenty-six years Colonel Margarethe Cammermeyer served proudly as a nurse for the United States Army. Her military record was spotless. She had cared for wounded soldiers in Vietnam and won numerous awards, including the 1985 Veterans Administration Nurse of the Year award.

She was finishing her doctorate in nursing and laying the groundwork to become one of the three highest-ranking nurses in the entire U.S. military when, on July 11, 1992, she was discharged after acknowledging to military personnel that she was a lesbian.

At the time, the Department of Defense had a regulation banning all gays and lesbians from serving in the military. The regulation stated that homosexuals were incompatible with military service because they adversely affected the ability of the military to maintain discipline, good order, and morale.

Margarethe Cammermeyer took her case to the courts, and in 1994 a federal judge declared the military's antigay policy unconstitutional and ordered that she be reinstated into the military. She has said, "I challenged an unjust regulation . . . so that all Americans' service to their country will be judged on the basis of performance, not prejudice."[1]

Margarethe Cammermeyer was born in March 1942 in Oslo, Norway. She was the eldest of four children. Hitler's armies had conquered Norway, and Margarethe's family lived in an apartment across the street from Nazi headquarters. Her parents were part of the underground anti-Nazi resistance. When Margarethe was only a few months old, her mother took her out for a ride in her baby carriage. Underneath the blankets, she'd hidden guns that she secretly handed off to members of the resistance.

As a girl Margarethe was impressed by the courage of the women working in the resistance and drawn to the idea of one day becoming a soldier. "Would I be woman enough . . . to do the hard job of fighting for country and freedom?" she asked herself. "Would I be able to choose the greater good over personal safety? Would I stand up—regardless of the cost—for what was right?"[2]

On May 8, 1945, the Allies liberated Oslo and, as Margarethe watched the American soldiers march through town, her heart was filled with gratitude and respect for the U.S. military.

In 1950 Margarethe's father was offered a job in Washington, D.C. He was a renowned scientist who studied the brain. A year later, the family secured permission from Norway to emigrate to the United States.

When Margarethe started elementary school in Washington, she was taller than all of her classmates. The school decided that even though she spoke no English, she should skip fourth grade and move on to fifth. Margarethe recalled that she felt "out of place, awkward, and stupid."[3]

Later she found that she could make friends through

sports. Margarethe became the president of her high school girls' athletic association and at fifteen was asked to join the Arcade Pontiac semiprofessional, fast-pitch softball team.

In the fall of 1959 Margarethe entered the University of Maryland hoping to become a doctor. In her first semester she took a rigorous pre-med schedule but spent more time socializing with friends than she did studying and was put on academic probation.

Near the end of her sophomore year, she was at a bowling party when a graduate from the Army Student Nurse Program walked in, proudly wearing her military uniform. Remembering the esteem she'd felt for women in the Norwegian Resistance, Margarethe realized that she too wanted to serve her new country as a military nurse.

In 1961 she joined the Army Student Nurse Program. She rose through the ranks to second lieutenant and graduated in 1963 after passing the two-day state board nursing examination. She was now ready to officially embark on her military career.

On July 24, 1963, the army sent her to Brooke Army Medical Center in Fort Sam Houston, Texas. There, she and other new nurses played war games in which soldiers would pretend to fight and suffer the sorts of ghoulish wounds that are common on the battlefield. They would apply makeup that made their wounds look authentic. "After three or four days," Margarethe recalled, "I learned to look without feeling, treat without thinking, and work without getting tired."[4]

After basic training, she worked in the gynecology and obstetrics ward of an army hospital in Georgia. In March of 1964 she was sent to work on a U.S. base in Nuremberg, Germany. While in Germany she met Harvey Hawken, a tank commander. They were married on August 14, 1965, in Nuremberg. At the time, it never occurred to Margarethe that she might be a lesbian.

Soon after the couple returned to the United States in

1966, Harvey was notified that he was to report for duty in Vietnam. The conflict over there was escalating. Margarethe immediately volunteered to be sent to Vietnam as well. She not only wanted to be nearer to her husband but also felt that it was her duty as a nurse to serve in combat and help the wounded.

Margarethe served in Vietnam from February 1967 to May 1968 during some of the war's most intense fighting, including the Tet offensive. As the head nurse of an intensive care ward, she said, "My work was a mix of contradictions. I helped save men with such massive injuries that I can only wonder if they hated me for it. When we did make them 100 percent better, we were the agents that propelled them back out into combat and possible death. When we couldn't save them, I was there with them when they died."[5]

When the head nurse of the neurosurgical unit at the hospital at Long Binh left, Margarethe took over her position. Here, most of her patients were recovering from severe brain or spinal injuries. Many were mute or comatose. Small changes, like the ability of a patient to suddenly blink his eyelid or twitch his finger, seemed like miracles.

When Margarethe and Harvey were finished with their tours of duty in Vietnam, they went to live on a beautiful piece of land they had bought near Puget Sound, in Washington State. They decided to start a family, and over the course of the next decade, Margarethe would be busy raising four sons, working as nurse at a military hospital, and taking graduate courses in nursing from the University of Washington.

The family was almost totally self-sufficient on their land. They raised their own vegetables, got eggs from their ducks, caught fish in their pond. "To our friends," Margarethe recalled, "we were the perfect couple. They admired how well we worked together and how much we were able to accomplish."[6]

However, tensions were rising in their marriage. Harvey resented how much time Margarethe was dedicating to her work. A family friend said that Harvey "was the old-fashioned type who wanted his wife to stay home and take care of the house and family."[7]

Finally, in 1980, Margarethe asked for a divorce. In August of that year a judge awarded Harvey custody of the children. Margarethe was devastated. After much soul-searching, however, she decided not to contest the decision. She felt that the court battle would become too nasty and that she had to spend much time at her work. "It had nothing to do with who loved them the most," she said. "But rather what was in their best interest."[8]

After taking a job at a veterans hospital in San Francisco, she was given the first Nurse of the Year award from the Veterans Administration in 1985. She was also named Bay Area Federal Employee of the Year and Woman of the Year by the Women's Veterans Association.

By 1987 Margarethe had moved back to Washington to be closer to her sons. She had been promoted to colonel and was the chief nurse of the Washington State National Guard. On the Fourth of July of that year, she met a university professor and artist named Diane Divelbess.

At the time of their introduction, Margarethe was still not aware of her sexual orientation, although she was aware that there was an emptiness in her life. She would later say, "My relationship with Diane evolved out of mutual caring, trust, respect, and enjoyment of being together. It just felt right, and that rightness made me realize I am a lesbian."[9]

Margarethe believed this was a purely personal realization that would in no way impact her busy work, and she began laying the groundwork to become the chief nurse of the entire National Guard. In order to do this, she had to attend War College. The work there would involve classified information so she would have to obtain a top-secret clearance. During the routine security clearance investigation, an agent of the Department of Defense asked her a question concerning homosexuality.

In the back of her mind, Margarethe had known that this might happen, but assumed that her position as colonel and her spotless military record would protect her. She also thought it was important to be honest about her sexual orientation so that she couldn't be blackmailed. She told the agent that she was a lesbian.

Later, she would say, "At the time . . . there was not much talk about gays in the military. I never thought I'd have to choose between being honest and serving my country. I didn't think I'd lose my military career because of prejudice and hate."[10]

The military's policy toward homosexuals has changed in almost every decade since World War I to conform to the prevailing social attitude toward homosexuality. In 1982 the policy was known as Regulation AR 135-175. It stated that a member shall be removed from the military if "the member has stated that he/she is a homosexual."[11] Between 1980 and 1990 more than 1,400 military personnel every year were discharged because of this regulation.

Seven months after Margarethe made the statement, she was informed that her security clearance had been withdrawn and that she was under consideration to be discharged. She began assembling a legal team, declaring, "I'm not a young private, and the Army can't beat up on me. They have to deal with the career that I have already served."[12]

By 1990 her lawyers were still waiting for the army to make a move. Margarethe was continuing to perform her work as chief nurse, and when the conflict in the Persian Gulf erupted, she volunteered to serve. Her unit, however, was not called up.

During this time, she also decided that it was important

for her to tell her sons that she was a lesbian. Although she was terrified that they would reject her or be ashamed of her, she wanted to warn them about the battle she was facing and the publicity it might attract. To her surprise, each boy told her that he already knew and that it was fine with him. Over the course of the next few years, all of her sons would come to live in the home she shared with Diane.

On March 18, 1991, she received a telegram stating that the army would recommend her discharge but that she would be given a chance to plead her case at an administrative hearing. Two days later, Margarethe received her doctorate in nursing.

Margarethe knew that her colleagues and patients would learn about the hearing and her sexual orientation. The day the news hit the papers, she sneaked in a back door of the veterans hospital but ran into a Vietnam vet she'd known for many years. He asked, "Greta, do you know what the most important thing is to an infantryman? A buddy. And you can be mine and share my foxhole with me anytime."[13] All day long well-wishers swamped her office, offering their support.

The day of the hearing was July 14, 1991—exactly thirty years after she had first been sworn in to the military. Margarethe's defense team hoped to demonstrate that the army's policy was irrational and based solely on prejudice. Further, her lawyers wanted to prove that there was a long history of gays and lesbians serving honorably in the military, whether or not the military wished to acknowledge this.

After outlining Margarethe's long list of accomplishments in the military, witnesses testified to her leadership abilities. They stated that even after her unit had learned about her sexual orientation, there had been no breakdown in morale or unit cohesion.

A former assistant secretary of defense talked at length about the 1988 Defense Personnel Security Research and Education Center (PERSEREC) Report. This report, commissioned by the Defense Department, concluded that the military's policy on homosexuals was based on stereotypical notions and prejudice.

The report found no evidence to support the claim that lesbians and gays were bad security risks. Nor did it find proof that gays disrupted order, discipline, or morale. The report went on to suggest that the policy should be eradicated.

An expert testified that the rationales that had once been used to keep blacks out of the army were the same ones being used today to keep gays out—including fear of a loss of unit cohesion and morale.

The last person to testify was Margarethe Cammermeyer. In her impeccably pressed dress uniform, her chest pinned with many medals, she stood and said, "There are times when change can be made only by someone stepping forth, being willing perhaps to expose themselves and their vulnerability so that others become aware of the fact that there are differences in the world. So that people will understand these differences are okay and don't affect our ability to be part of an organization or to make a contribution. And so, I choose . . . to come before you and my family, and be vulnerable in hopes that perhaps it can influence making a change and allowing us to serve as we have in the past and will continue to do in the future."[14]

After an hour of deliberation, the board announced it had reached a decision. It stated, "Colonel Cammermeyer has proved to be a great asset [to the military] and the medical profession as a whole. She has consistently provided superb leadership. . . . Notwithstanding, the board finds Colonel Margarethe Cammermeyer is a homosexual."[15] It recommended she be discharged.

On June 11, 1992, her last day in the military, Margarethe Cammermeyer handed in a three-hundred-page book she had written, which would become the definitive document on standard operating procedures for military nurses. Then she handed over her identification cards and said good-bye to her staff. The tall, straight-backed colonel fought back tears as she said good-bye to friends and colleagues. She was the highest-ranking officer ever to be discharged under the military's antigay policy.

Reporters from across the country were eagerly waiting to interview her. Although a naturally private person, Margarethe felt it was her duty to speak out against the military's unjust policy and to do anything she could to sway public opinion. She began appearing on talk shows and television programs. She said that as she fielded questions "from people who proudly repeated ignorant and malicious antigay phrases, I was struck by the fact that homophobia is one of the last socially acceptable prejudices in America. . . . That permission to hate those who are 'different,' I was beginning to see, is additionally fueled by the military's policy of discrimination."[16]

In 1992 a report from the General Accounting Office of the U.S. government came out detailing the cost of this policy. Between 1980 and 1991 the government spent $494 million to train and then discharge homosexuals. This did not include the cost of investigations. In 1990 the cost of investigations against gays was more than $2.5 million.

Margarethe vowed to battle the policy in civil court. She stated, "The symbolism of the government's saying you are unworthy to defend your country is powerful. It's just one step away from being told you're unworthy to vote, you're unworthy to be hired, you're unworthy to live where you want to live."[17]

While she was preparing her case, Bill Clinton was elected president in 1992. He contacted Margarethe and told her that he hoped to lift the ban on gays serving in the military. In 1993 he began making good on this promise by pushing for the Congress to reexamine the military's policy. Margarethe flew to Washington, D.C., and met individually with more than fifty senators, urging them to study the facts in the PERSEREC report and to vote to lift the ban on gays. Senator Sam Nunn of the Senate Armed Services Committee held hearings on the subject, and in the spring of 1993 Margarethe testified before this committee.

It became clear that there would not be enough votes in Congress to support ending the ban. Instead, the Clinton administration announced that it would agree to a compromise, which became known as the "don't ask, don't tell policy." Recruits and military members seeking security clearances would no longer be asked about their sexual orientation. However, if any of them disclosed that they were gay, they could be investigated and discharged.

In the spring of 1994 Margarethe's case was tried before the federal district court in Seattle. On June 1, the judge found in her favor and ordered that she be reinstated to the military. He stated that the antigay regulation under which she had been discharged was "based solely on prejudice. Prejudice, whether founded on unsubstantiated fears, cultural myths, stereotypes or erroneous assumptions cannot be the basis of a discriminatory classification."[18] This decision affected only the military's old regulation, which had been the basis for her dismissal and did not relate to the newer "don't ask, don't tell" policy.

When Margarethe reported back to the National Guard in July of 1994, her unit met her with a standing ovation. The federal government is currently appealing the federal court decision.

In 1992 Margarethe published a book about her experiences called *Serving in Silence*, which was also made into a television movie starring Glenn Close. She said she felt that it was her responsibility to tell her story and "to show that our lives were full, to show that 'Yes, not only am I a lesbian, but I have a very loving, caring family. . . . Let me introduce you to my kids, my grandkids, and my partner, and see how different that is from your own life.'"[19]

Today, she lives with Diane and her youngest son, Andy, in Washington State. In her free time, she travels around the country speaking to colleges and high schools. She has also become the "Dear Abby" for gays in the military, who contact her through E-mail, asking her for advice and support.

"I believe my journey has been a spiritual journey," she has said. "I believe in finding meaning in the worst adversity. This is what has helped me get from one point to another, and what shows me what I'm supposed to do next."[20]

TWO

≈

Marian Wright Edelman

On June 1, 1996, a "Stand for Children" march and rally brought together an estimated 200,000 supporters at the Lincoln Memorial in Washington, D.C. Giant banners proclaiming *Leave No Child Behind* were draped on either side of the monument. The rally's organizer, Marian Wright Edelman, is one of our nation's leading children's rights crusaders. She hoped the event would remind politicians on Capitol Hill and across the country that while spending cuts in welfare and other benefit programs might be popular with voters, the impact of these cuts ultimately will be felt by America's poor and disadvantaged children. She declared, "The world's richest nation lets 2,600 children be born every day into poverty. We have the biggest wallet in the industrialized world, but we have a much smaller will to share it with our children."[1]

Marian Wright Edelman has dedicated her life to fighting on behalf of America's children. She has said, "I'm doing what I think I was put on this earth to do. And I'm really grateful to have something that I'm passionate about and that I think is profoundly important."[2]

Marian Wright was born on June 6, 1939, the youngest of five children. Her father was the pastor of the Shiloh Baptist Church in Bennetsville, South Carolina. He and Marian's mother strongly believed in education, and every evening they would gather their children around the dinner table where the youngsters did their homework. Marian's brother recalled that if they had no assignments, their father would say, "'Well, assign yourself.'. . . It was just read, read, read."[3]

Bennetsville's African-American community was very tight-knit, and Marian remembered that the adults she knew "made children feel valued and important. . . . And while life was often hard and resources scarce, we always knew who we were and that the measure of our worth was inside our heads and hearts and not outside in our possessions or on our backs."[4]

The strong and supportive bonds of the African-American community could not, however, shield children like Marian from the harsh realities of racism that were prevalent in the larger society. At the time, the South was segregated and blacks were treated as second-class citizens. Marian found it absurd that she was not allowed to use the same drinking fountain as white children and was outraged at being barred from using the public swimming pool. In the sixth grade she wrote an essay entitled "Barriers of Racial Injustice Do Not Have to Be Insurmountable," which she read aloud to her school assembly.

Her parents taught her that no matter how unjust racism might be, it was not an excuse to keep from succeeding in life. In high school, Marian was a hardworking overachiever who, as one friend recalled, "always read the whole book when the class was asked to read one chapter."[5] After graduating as class valedictorian in 1956, Marian attended the all-black Spelman College in Atlanta, Georgia.

At first she considered a career in the foreign service and in her junior year won a scholarship to study in Geneva, Switzerland. During the second semester abroad she spent two months in the Soviet Union. She found that there was far less racism in Europe than there was in America's South. In Europe, she could go into any restaurant and be served, and she was not forced to sit at the back of buses.

When she returned to Spelman for her senior year, she felt that she was seeing her country with new eyes and that she could no longer tolerate living under segregation. She was ready to fight. So were many others. At the time, the Spelman campus was abuzz with stories of the increasingly powerful civil rights movement.

In February 1960, four African-American students in Greensboro, North Carolina, had sat down at a Woolworth's lunch counter and refused to leave even after they were informed that they would not be served because they were black. The idea of the nonviolent "sit-in" quickly spread to other cities, and on March 15, 1960, Marian joined one of the largest sit-ins in Atlanta.

Marian was among two hundred students who simultaneously converged at numerous eating places in the city's public buildings and sat down at the counters and tables. She was one of fourteen students arrested. This experience led her to conclude that instead of going into the foreign service she would enter the law, believing it would be the most useful tool in fighting segregation.

After graduating valedictorian from Spelman, she won a scholarship to Yale Law School. When she finished her studies, she opened a law office in Jackson, Mississippi, and became the first black woman lawyer in the state. At the time, Mississippi had a larger proportion of black people than any other state and many of the poorest black people in the nation. It was one of the states in which a group called the Student Nonviolent Coordinating Committee (SNCC) had started a voter registration drive to encourage blacks to use their vote and elect politicians who would fairly represent them. The success of the voter registration drive ignited the hatred of Mississippi's Ku Klux Klan, which began to retaliate with cross burnings and acts of violence.

When Marian opened her law office in 1964, the state was about to become the focal point of the Freedom Summer. Groups of civil rights organizations were coming together to send volunteers to Mississippi to work on voter registration and other projects.

At the start of the summer, three young Freedom Summer workers were jailed and then released by the sheriff to the KKK, which murdered them. It was clear that the danger was escalating. Over the course of that hot, humid summer, twenty-seven black churches would be burned, eighty civil rights workers were beaten, and one thousand were arrested. Marian worked around the clock trying to get these people out of jail.

She said, "That summer I very seldom got a client out of jail who had not been beaten by white police officers, who didn't have bones broken or teeth missing."[6] She knew that because of her work on their behalf, she could easily become a target for violence. She recalled that she never started her car "without leaving the driver's-side door open. That way . . . if a bomb was planted under the hood and exploded, there was a chance of being thrown out and escaping death."[7]

The violence was disturbing, but so was the poverty she witnessed. She saw children who were starving or sick, others who were illiterate because they had to work all day in the fields instead of attending school. How, Marian wondered, could America, the wealthiest nation in the world, allow its children to suffer in such poverty?

This was a question that President Lyndon Johnson was asking as well. In 1964 he declared a national war on poverty. One program was called Head Start. Federal funds were allocated to provide centers to serve the basic health, nutritional, and educational needs of disadvantaged pre-school-age children. A number of civic groups and churches that were interested in helping Mississippi's children formed the Child Development Group of Mississippi (CDGM) to write proposals for Head Start funds.

Despite her hectic schedule, Marian served on the board. In a few weeks eighty-six Head Start centers were set up across the state. One important outcome of these programs was that parents who before had felt powerless were suddenly demanding more control and improvements in their local schools.

CDGM, however, was continually forced to battle racist state leaders to win funding for the programs. Through these confrontations, Marian emerged as the group's most articulate and visionary leader. In March 1967, she testified at a public hearing on poverty. "People are starving," she said. "There is absolutely nothing for them to do . . . I wish the senators would have a chance to go around and just look at the empty cupboards in the [Mississippi] Delta and the number of people who are going around begging just to feed their children."[8]

In April 1967 Marian took Senator Robert Kennedy and his aide, Peter Edelman, on a tour of Mississippi's poor. Kennedy said that his heart broke when he tickled a hungry child and could not arouse even a smile from him. He later returned to Washington invigorated to do even more to end hunger in the United States.

But by the end of 1967 the nation's focus had shifted from the war on poverty to the war in Vietnam. Marian felt that too much money was being spent fighting an unpopular war overseas when people were dying at home. She heard the civil rights leader Martin Luther King, Jr., state that the United States was spending $50,000 for every enemy killed in Vietnam but only $53 for every poor person at home.[9] She was encouraged that he wanted to refocus the nation's attention on the poor by asking poor people to come and camp out in Washington, D.C. That way the government could no longer ignore them. Throughout the early part of 1968 Marian took part in helping plan the march.

In March of 1968 she decided it would be easier for her to do this work if she lived in Washington. The city had another appeal: Kennedy's aide, Peter Edelman, lived there. Marian had stayed in contact with Peter, who was white and Jewish, and she felt that they had a great deal in common, including their commitment to the poor.

The spring of 1968 was filled with much sadness and shock. On April 4 Martin Luther King, Jr., was assassinated. Marian knew that he would have wanted the poor people's campaign to go on so she pushed ahead in her work.

By mid-May the poor had begun arriving from all over the country on buses and in mule trains and crowded, run-down cars. Tents for 3,000 were set up in the park across from the Reflecting Pool and near the White House.

The encampment became known as Resurrection City. For a month the poor lived there as it rained steadily and the ground turned to mud. The city began to resent the mess and litter the encampment was creating. And then, on June 6, Senator Robert Kennedy was assassinated. With two of their strongest advocates dead, the protesters were plunged into despair.

On June 24 Resurrection City was disbanded. The campaign had succeeded in winning only a few small victories, including more money budgeted for food programs. While the campaign had not been as successful as Marian had hoped, she said that she had no intention of giving up the struggle. "I

don't think anybody ever has the right to give up on children or give up on the poor," she said. "The needs remain. The needs grow."[10]

On July 14, 1968, Marian and Peter Edelman were married. It was the first known interracial marriage in the state of Virginia since the Supreme Court struck down a law making such marriages illegal in June 1967. After their honeymoon, Marian worked at the Washington Research Project studying the use of government money designed to help educate the poor. Her groundbreaking report found that most of the money was not going to the children, and her results made headlines in the *Washington Post*.

In 1971 she helped draft a child development bill that would give more funding to Head Start. Although it passed through both houses of Congress, it was vetoed by President Richard Nixon. Frustrated, Marian said, "Everyone loves children. . . . But when [politicians] get into the budget rooms, or behind closed doors—to really decide how they're going to carve up money—children get lost in the process because they are not powerful."[11] She decided that from then on she would fight for the nation's poor children.

In 1971 the Edelmans moved to Boston, where Peter became vice president of a state university. By then they had two sons, and in 1974 their third son would be born. Marian worked at Harvard but continued to fly to Washington to work at the Research Project on the needs of poor children. In 1973 she won funds to start the Children's Defense Fund (CDF). The goal of this organization was to "provide systematic and long-term assistance to children and to make their needs an important matter of public policy."[12]

One of the CDF's lawyers and later the chair of the board of directors was Hillary Rodham, who would later become a powerful advocate of the organization as the nation's First Lady and wife of President Bill Clinton. Under Marian's lead-

ership throughout the 1970s, the CDF won increased funding for programs that helped children. But when President Ronald Reagan was elected in 1980, his administration began slashing funding for welfare and domestic programs. Many of the CDF's gains were lost.

Marian refused to be discouraged and began meeting regularly with legislators, lobbying for their support. She always had reams of statistics at her disposal. "A black infant in Chicago," she might say, "is more likely to die in the first year of life than an infant in Cuba or Costa Rica."[13] She wanted to highlight just how far the United States lagged behind other countries in taking care of its children. In 1981 the CDF also began to issue an annual report titled "A Children's Defense Budget," which clearly outlined problems facing the nation's poor children and suggested solutions.

By 1983 teen pregnancy was becoming a major problem in America, especially in black communities. The mothers of these children, the CDF found, would earn about half the lifetime income of a woman who waited until the age of twenty to have her first child. "I saw from our own statistics," Marian said, "that 55.5 percent of all black babies were born out of wedlock, a great many of them to teenage girls. It just hit me over the head—that this situation insured black child poverty for the next generation."[14]

To try to address the problem, Marian and the CDF launched a nationwide campaign to discourage teens from becoming pregnant. They printed eye-catching posters and made public announcements for television and radio stations. Marian also established the Pregnancy Prevention Clearing House, an agency that offered information and technical assistance to pregnancy-prevention programs all over the country.

Throughout the 1980s the CDF increased in influence and size, employing over one hundred staff members. Marian became a well-known public figure. In 1983 *Ladies' Home Journal* elected her one of the one hundred most influential women in America. In 1987 a book of her lectures was published.

As the nation began to focus on the problems of young people in our society, 1988 was declared the Year of the Child. After a year of in-depth study, the CDF wrote a bill called the Act for Better Child Care (ABC). This bill called for $2.5 billion to help bring increased aid to families and children. By the summer, the bill was being deliberated in Congress. Throughout her years working at the CDF, Marian had established a powerful network of support all over the country. Legislators suddenly found themselves inundated with calls and mail from their constituents, as well as letters and drawings from children, urging them to support the bill.

It seemed that the bill would pass, but at the last minute two of the bill's strongest supporters shocked everyone by withdrawing their support. The bill did not pass and Marian was furious. After she fired off angry letters to the two senators, and sent copies to newspapers, one observer declared, "She basically kicked her allies in the face."[15] But Marian made it clear she did not want allies who would turn their back on her when she needed them.

In 1990 Congress eventually passed a bill that allocated less than the approximately $1 billion that the original ABC bill called for. Nevertheless, Marian saw this as a victory for poor children across the country.

When Bill Clinton was elected president in 1992, Marian knew that she had a strong friend and ally in the First Lady and the president. She saw them as "an extraordinary pair [who understand that children's issues are] . . . something that is central to the security and economic well-being of America."[16]

In the first year of the Clinton administration, Marian and the CDF fought for some important gains for poor children.

She pushed Congress to pass bills approving an increase in the Earned Income Tax Credit (which gave additional monetary support to working parents), the Childhood Hunger Prevention Act (which helped poor families with the expense of housing and food), the Family and Medical Leave Act (which enabled working parents to take twelve weeks' unpaid leave to help care for a sick family member). Congress also increased funding for immunizing children and for Head Start programs.

In the fall of 1996 a conservative Congress began fighting for a welfare reform bill that would give lump grants to states to distribute to the poor in aid programs of their own devising. Having witnessed the misuse of state funds for Head Start in Mississippi in the 1960s, Marian worried that the welfare reform bill might eliminate the safety net of protections for poor children. She urged President Clinton not to sign the bill, stating, "This President of all Presidents knows what it will mean. . . . There are fifteen million children living in poverty in this country today . . . [and] the so-called welfare-reform plan would push 1.2 million more of them into poverty."[17]

When Clinton signed the welfare reform bill in August of 1996, Marian denounced him for what she called a "moment of shame" and making "a mockery of his pledge not to hurt children."[18] The next month Peter Edelman resigned in protest from his position as acting assistant secretary of health and human services.

Throughout her career Marian Wright Edelman has been accused of believing that the solution to poverty is through the expenditure of federal money. Opponents say that there are too many examples of the failure of the federal government to solve people's problems and that individual communities and states are better equipped to solve their own problems. Edelman's response to such criticism is that "where you can see a general need everywhere, you try to have a national solution."[19]

Marian Wright Edelman has won many awards and honorary degrees. In 1985 she became a MacArthur Foundation Prize Fellow, and in 1988 won the Albert Schweitzer Humanitarian Award. In 1992 she wrote the best-selling book *The Measure of Our Success: A Letter to My Children and Yours*.

She has said, "When I fight about what is happening to other people's children, I'm doing that because I want to leave a community and a world that is better than the one I found."[20]

THREE

MYRLIE EVERS-WILLIAMS

On the evening of July 11, 1963, Myrlie Evers heard a car arriving and knew that her husband, Medgar, was home. She sighed with relief. He was one of the leaders of the National Association for the Advancement of Colored People (NAACP) and had been receiving death threats for his work to bring civil rights to Mississippi. Before Medgar could open the front door, the stillness of the night was shattered by gunfire.

Myrlie ran to him as he lay face down, blood pouring from the fatal wound in his chest. Myrlie Evers vowed that her husband's death would not be in vain.

Twenty-two years later, on February 18, 1995, she became the first woman to serve as chair for the NAACP. Despite the strides that have been made in fighting discrimination since her husband's murder, Evers-Williams still sees much work to be done. She has said, "I see the same challenges of the past with us, maybe cloaked a little differently. We are still plagued with racism. We still find discrimination in the job market, in education and housing. I have faced discrimination not only due to the color of my skin, but also because I am female. . . . But we keep a-comin'. Strong as we've always been, more aware of ourselves, our strength, and power potential, willing to take more risks."[1]

When Myrlie Louise Beasley was born on March 17, 1933, in Vicksburg, Mississippi, her mother was only sixteen years old. Soon after giving birth, she separated from Myrlie's father and left Myrlie in the care of her paternal grandmother and her widowed aunt, Myrlie Polk. She would later state, "I can recall only warmth and love and protectiveness from all of the people around me. Nor did it seem strange to me as I grew up that my mother did not live with me. I had an identity as Mrs. Beasley's granddaughter and Mrs. Polk's niece."[2]

Both her aunt and her grandmother, whom she called Mama, were schoolteachers, and they put a high value on education. Myrlie strove to make them proud by being an excellent student and piano player.

Although Mama and Aunt Myrlie tried to protect her from the injustice of racial discrimination, it was impossible to escape it in the segregated South. When Myrlie went into town, there were separate rest rooms and drinking fountains for whites and blacks. Myrlie was banned from using certain, white-only, libraries. She recalled the frustration and absurdity of being forced to sit in the back of buses. "Often the seats in the Negro section would be filled and we would be jammed together standing in the aisle behind the sign, while the front of the bus would be all but deserted."[3]

Myrlie graduated from high school second in her class and said that in the graduating speeches "no one hinted that in our graduating class there might be a future President of the United States, a future senator, a future governor. And no one said that our achievements would be limited only by our desires and our willingness to work for what we wanted. No one could. For all of us understood, in our bones if not in our minds, that we were Negroes and that this was Mississippi."[4]

In 1950 Myrlie entered Alcorn A & M College in Loman, Mississippi. Mama and Aunt Myrlie dropped her off with strict instructions to study hard and not pay any attention to the older boys who would be returning to school after serving in World War II. But on her first day, Myrlie noticed a handsome veteran who was also the school's football star. His name was Medgar Evers.

After dating for a year, the couple were married on Christmas Eve of 1951, against the wishes of Mama and Aunt Myrlie. The wedding was a series of disasters—Myrlie broke out in a rash, Medgar lost her ring, Mama was so mad she would hardly speak to either one of them. Nevertheless, in their wedding pictures, the couple looked happy and hopeful.

The next year, Medgar finished his studies and was recruited to work as a life insurance salesman for a black-owned company. Despite Mama's protestations, Myrlie quit school to follow her husband to the miserable swampy town of Mound Bayou, Mississippi. She went to work as a secretary in her husband's office.

Medgar was always out on the road trying to sell life and funeral insurance to black families, including those who were sharecropping on the large plantations. Day after day, he would return from his ventures to tell Myrlie horror stories about the poverty he had witnessed. He saw families living in tar-paper shacks, children on the verge of starvation, men and women who had never learned to read. In an attempt to try to help these people, he began working for the NAACP.

The NAACP was founded in 1908 by three white persons—a Jew, a Southerner, and the granddaughter of an abolitionist—to try to right the wrongs done to blacks. By the beginning of World War II the NAACP had 85,000 members. Only about 10 percent were whites, but most of them served in executive roles. Throughout the 1950s and 1960s more blacks would move into leadership positions in the NAACP as it became one of the leading organizations in the fight for civil rights.

The Mississippi branch of the NAACP wanted to expand, and Medgar was offered a job as field secretary. By this time, Myrlie Evers had given birth to their first child, a boy, named Darrell Kenyatta Evers. The family moved to Jackson, Mississippi, where once again Myrlie served as her husband's secretary, researching his speeches and welcoming visiting civil rights workers. She also gave birth to two more children.

From the start, she said, "We lived with death as a constant companion 24 hours a day. Medgar knew what the risks were. He just decided that he had to do what he had to do. But I knew at some point in time he would be taken from me."[5]

By 1961 Medgar was leading economic boycotts of Jackson's businesses, which refused to hire black workers and would not allow black patrons to try on the clothes they bought. Myrlie recalled, "In the Jackson newspapers there were editorials calling for 'a flow of blood' on the streets, pinpointing Medgar as someone something should be 'done' about."[6]

By mid-July the movement was so strong that a letter was sent to the governor demanding an end to racial discrimination in the city's parks, stores, schools, and accommodations. The mayor responded by telling blacks, "You are treated, no matter what anybody else tells you, with dignity, courtesy and respect. . . . Refuse to pay any attention to any of these outside agitators."[7] Medgar Evers went on television rebutting the mayor's outrageous statement and in a speech of great forcefulness outlined the case for desegregation.

After this, when Myrlie would pick up the ringing phone, on the other end would be a racist spewing a stream of invectives at her and her husband. A firebomb was thrown at their house. Myrlie and Medgar taught their children to stay away from the windows and to dive to the floor if they heard gunshots. Then, on the night that President John Kennedy gave a civil rights address to the country, Medgar was shot.

Devastated and angry, Myrlie thought, "I'm going to make whoever did this pay."[8]

Medgar's assassin was a white supremacist named Byron De La Beckwith. At his first trial, in 1964, Myrlie recalled, "While I was testifying, the Governor, Ross Barnett, walked in—I'll never forget this—and he paused and looked at me, turned and went to Beckwith, shook his hand, slapped him on the shoulder and sat down next to him. He was sending a clear signal to the jurors that this man was to be acquitted."[9]

Indeed, in both this trial and in a subsequent one, the all-white juries deadlocked and Beckwith was set free. Undeterred, Myrlie vowed that one day she would make certain that her husband's murderer was behind bars.

She also knew she had to continue her own life and do what was best for their children, who were ages three, eight, and nine. Medgar had died thousands of dollars in debt, but the NAACP told her that if she would make appearances on his behalf, they would continue to pay his $6,100-a-year salary. Myrlie agreed and every weekend was away making speeches. Not surprisingly, her eldest son began to worry that she too would be shot. It was becoming increasingly obvious to Myrlie that her family could not heal while they were living in the house where Medgar had been shot. "There was nowhere in Mississippi I wanted to live," she recalled. "Medgar and I had always talked about how, if we ever left the state, we'd go to California."[10]

Myrlie and the children moved to Claremont, California, outside of Los Angeles. There, Myrlie enrolled in Pomona College to finish her degree and continued giving speeches for the NAACP. In 1967 she published a biography of her life with Medgar and his work for the NAACP called *For Us, The Living*. In 1983 the book would be made into a television movie.

After graduating with a degree in sociology in 1968, Myr

lie was hired by the college as a development director. Two years later, when Congressman Glenard P. Lipscomb died in February of 1970, Myrlie decided to run for his office. She said that her reason for running was to push for greater racial tolerance. "As a nation," she said, "we are dividing up into separate groups and pulling ourselves apart. . . . Those who say integration is not a realistic idea might be right, but I will hope and pray and work to show they are incorrect."[11]

She was running as a Democrat in a heavily Republican district. Her opponent was a former officer of the ultraconservative John Birch Society who was calling for deep cuts in spending for the social programs that Myrlie supported. During the campaign, she received hate mail and death threats. Although she lost, she won 36 percent of the vote, which was more than any other Democratic candidate in the district had received in more than a decade.

In the early part of the 1970s Myrlie worked as a contributing editor for *Ladies' Home Journal* and for two years served as a vice president of an advertising firm. In 1975 she became the director of community affairs for the Atlantic Richfield Company, using her position to lobby for money for organizations such as the National Women's Education Fund.

During this time, she also met and fell in love with Walter Williams, a retired longshoreman and union activist. They were married in 1976. She said, "There were many people who thought I should not remarry, that I should be an eternal widow. But Walter gave me tremendous love and was strong enough to deal with Medgar's presence in my life."[12]

In 1987 she was appointed by Los Angeles Mayor Tom Bradley as the city's first black female commissioner of the Board of Public Works. She was in charge of overseeing everything from trash removal to street maintenance. She had approximately six thousand employees working for her and a budget of hundreds of millions of dollars.

Myrlie had stayed in touch with officials in Mississippi

throughout the years since Medgar's death to keep the case against Beckwith alive. The first real breakthrough came in 1989 when a journalist began investigating the Mississippi Sovereignty Commission, a secret agency that throughout the 1950s and 1960s was possibly connected with jury tampering, including the jury in Beckwith's second trial. Myrlie pushed for a retrial. Finally, on February 5, 1994, she saw a racially mixed jury convict the man who had murdered her husband and send him to jail.

Almost exactly a year later, on February 7, 1995, she announced her bid to run for the chair of the NAACP. The venerable organization was in a state of turmoil that many felt was the worst in its long history. In August 1994 the executive director had been dismissed for using NAACP funds to settle a sexual harassment suit against him. In January 1995 the incumbent chairman was accused of misusing $1.4 million of NAACP funds. During his decade-long tenure, he had managed to allow the group to slide about $4 million into debt.

Although Walter Williams was ill with cancer and dying, Myrlie campaigned with his blessings. She said, "I love the NAACP. I believe it must survive. I believe it must thrive."[13] She also wanted to bring an end to the sexism within the organization, stating that "women are mostly on the very soft committees where no major decisions are made that directly impact the operation of the organization. The women of the association are more than ready to assert themselves and to call the hand of those males who have not guarded the association as carefully as they should have."[14]

Many in the NAACP saw her as the organization's best hope for salvation. Her life and work were a bridge between the turbulent protests of the 1950s and 1960s, while her experience as businesswoman and administrator gave her the necessary credentials to lead the NAACP in the 1990s.

One reporter stated, "Evers-Williams generates . . . goodwill and admiration. . . . In her Ferragamo pumps and gold buttoned suit, she glides through gritty confrontations in a private vessel of pure calm."[15]

In February 1995 Myrlie Evers-Williams was elected by a single-vote margin to be the new chair of an organization boasting 500,000 members with 2,200 branches across the country. "Duty beckons me," she told the members. "I am strong. Test me and you will see."[16]

Two days after her election, she got a call telling her that her husband was gravely ill. She flew home in time to hold him as he became unconscious. He died the next morning. Ten days later Myrlie had eye surgery but was back at work almost at once, ignoring both her physical and emotional pain.

Her first goal as chairwoman was to bring financial stability to the organization and to erase the multi-million-dollar debt. She cut the staff and hired a new financial officer. Then she began fund-raising, crisscrossing the country. Sometimes she visited as many as fifteen cities a week. The number of members sending in dues increased dramatically after her election. By April of 1995 she announced that $2 million had been pledged to the NAACP.

In addition to working to right the organization's finances, Myrlie Evers-Williams wanted the NAACP to take the lead in fighting the 1994 Republican-led Congress, which aimed to slash social programs, cut welfare, and abolish affirmative action. She saw their agenda as an attack on the hard-fought gains blacks had made since the 1950s.

"The area that worries me most is the mean-spiritedness and utter determination to roll back the clock," she said. "This is a Congress that is arrogant when it comes to race relations and unkind when painting a portrait of welfare mothers." She added that she felt it is "pure, unadulterated racism," when lawmakers contend that black women are the majority of welfare recipients. "If you look at the government statistics," she said, "the majority are Caucasian."[17]

In the future, she wants to reach out to young people of

all races. She hopes to go on the Internet to spread the message that "today, as yesterday, the combination of nonviolence and action is the only way to enjoy the civil right to a civilized society."[18] Further, she wants young people to remember that "if you are an African American and you feel you have been discriminated against, what is the first organization you tend to come to? [The NAACP.]"[19]

In February 1996 Myrlie faced a reelection campaign. She was challenged for her seat by a group led by the former chairman she had ousted a year earlier. Many saw this as a test of her leadership.

Myrlie Evers-Williams was not only reelected to a second term, but the candidates she backed swept board elections. In a progress-report speech to the group, Myrlie announced that under her leadership, the NAACP had ended 1995 with a cash surplus for the first time in six years. She predicted that with her spending cuts, the overall deficit would be reduced to $776,000 by 1997. She also announced gains in membership and plans for recruiting 500,000 new members. At the end of her speech, supporters were stamping their feet and shouting "Myrlie! Myrlie! Myrlie!"

In February 1996 a new executive director, Kweisi Mfume, was appointed. Mfume was a respected Democratic representative from Maryland and former head of the Congressional Black Caucus. In a speech at the NAACP's annual meeting, Mfume told the energized group, "Go tell it on the mountain that the NAACP is back. We will change this America that we love because we will change ourselves."[20]

Side by side, Mfume and Evers-Williams are hoping to lead the NAACP to a bright new future. She has said, "I do not intend to stay in this position for a lifetime, but I want to leave knowing that we have found a way to attract people who didn't go through the fire in the 1950s and 1960s to join the NAACP. I want to leave this organization healthy, knowing it can make a real difference in their lives."[21]

FOUR

~

ELIZABETH GLASER

For a while, Elizabeth Glaser felt like she had everything she could ever want in the world—a job she enjoyed, a famous television-star husband, and two children whom she adored. But in 1985, her four-year-old daughter, Ariel, was diagnosed with HIV, the virus that causes AIDS. Doctors determined that Elizabeth had contracted the virus during a blood transfusion and that she had unwittingly passed the disease to Ariel during breast-feeding. Her one-year-old son, Jake, was also infected. The only member of the family who did not have the virus was Elizabeth's husband, Paul.

Elizabeth discovered that ignorance and indifference were as big an enemy to children with AIDS as the disease itself. She felt that many leaders within the federal government were not aware of the growing number of children living with AIDS and that they were not allocating enough money to fund research focusing specifically on children with the disease. Further, she found that fear and misinformation led some people to unjustly treat children with HIV as if they were lepers, ostracizing them from their friends, their schools, their communities.

Elizabeth Glaser became a champion of equality who worked tirelessly to promote the rights of children stricken with AIDS. She firmly believed that such children must not be neglected in the war against this dread disease. Her dedication to this cause led her to establish the Pediatric AIDS Foundation, which would raise research money and educate the public about AIDS-infected girls and boys.

She said, "I am active in fighting AIDS because I want to be a person [Ari, who died in 1988] would be proud of. . . . In my weaker moments, I think about her courage and I am able to go on."[1]

Elizabeth Meyer was born on November 11, 1947. Her father was a businessman and her mother an urban renewal planner. The family lived in Hewlitt Harbor, a suburb on Long Island in New York State. In high school Elizabeth was a superb athlete.

She attended the University of Wisconsin, majoring in psychology, then earned a master's degree in early childhood education from Boston University. A year later she married her first husband, Hank Koransky. Elizabeth took a job as a teacher with Head Start, a program for disadvantaged preschoolers, in Boulder, Colorado. After two years the marriage dissolved and Elizabeth moved to Los Angeles. In 1973 she became a reading and social studies teacher at a private school, the Center for Early Childhood Education. "I never imagined that teaching could be so much fun," Elizabeth recalled.[2]

In 1975 Elizabeth started dating an actor named Paul Michael Glaser. He played the lead role of Starsky in a popular television detective show called *Starsky and Hutch*. On August 24, 1980, Elizabeth and he were married in a simple ceremony. Soon after, Elizabeth realized that she was pregnant. "All the goodness in the world seemed to be ours," she said. "In nine months I would have what I had always wanted most in the world, a child of my own with a man that I loved."[3]

During her pregnancy, Elizabeth took a new job as the educational director for the Los Angeles Children's Museum. She loved developing creative ideas for exciting hands-on exhibits such as Grandma's Attic, in which children could learn what life was like in pioneer days by playing with toys and trying on clothes from that era.

On August 4, 1981, she gave birth to their daughter, Ariel. Soon after the delivery, Elizabeth hemorrhaged and doctors gave her a blood transfusion. One of the seven pints she received that day was infected with HIV, although it would be years before Elizabeth would notice any symptoms of illness. (Today all hospitals test blood for the virus.)

On October 25, 1984, Elizabeth gave birth to their second child, Jake. Ten months after Jake was born, Paul was offered a job directing his first feature film.

A little less than a year later, in September of 1985, Ari who was starting preschool, began complaining of stomach cramps. She was also unusually tired. The doctors thought she must have some sort of mild infection and were not very concerned. But one afternoon, her lips turned a chalky white. Elizabeth was frightened. What was wrong with her daughter?

She took Ari to see a specialist, and he did a number of blood tests, which showed that her red blood cell count was dangerously low. (Red blood cells carry oxygen.) She was given a blood transfusion and gradually began to improve, although she never felt entirely well.

From January to April of 1986, Ari underwent a battery of tests aimed at determining the underlying cause of her illness. Each time Elizabeth had to call the hospital to get results from the tests, she would brace herself for bad news.

Each time the doctors would tell her that they still did not know what was wrong with Ari.

Finally, the doctors decided they should test for AIDS. Paul and Elizabeth figured that this disease would also be ruled out. But the next day, the doctor telephoned them and said that there was something odd about the results and that Ari would have to be tested again.

It had to be a mistake, Paul and Elizabeth assured each other. But the second test came back positive. "I remember walking into the bathroom and screaming as loud as I could," Elizabeth said. "Ari and Jake must have been out of the house because I would never have fallen apart in front of them. I was screaming and crying. I don't remember how long I stayed there. I don't remember anything."[4]

The rest of the family were tested, and it was discovered that Elizabeth and Jake were also infected with the virus. Elizabeth was terrified. She and her children were infected with a horrible virus for which there was no cure. The future that had seemed so bright was suddenly pitch dark. How, she wondered, could everything have gone so wrong so quickly?

"It was as if a hurricane had just come through town and completely demolished our home," Elizabeth recalled. "While all the pieces were there, they were upside down, sideways. Everything was strangely there but out of place."[5]

The doctors informed Elizabeth that the law required her to tell Ari's school that her daughter was HIV-positive. Elizabeth recalled stories she'd read in the newspaper about the horrible discrimination and hatred inflicted on other children with the disease. For example, there was the story of the Ray family from Florida. The three Ray children had been infected with HIV during blood transfusions and were subsequently barred from attending school. The family had successfully sued to have the children readmitted, and during the children's first week back in school their house was burned down.

Fearing that if she told the truth about Ari her daughter

would be forced to leave school, Elizabeth decided to avoid any possible confrontation by pulling her out immediately. There were only three weeks left before summer vacation, and she told the school that the doctors had recommended that Ari take some time off to recuperate from her stomach bug. She and Paul knew, however, that they could not, in good conscience, avoid telling the parents of Ari's friends.

One by one they called up the parents and told them they had something very important to discuss. They gave them the information that was available at the time—that there were no known cases of people passing the disease on through casual contact. The only known way of getting HIV was through intimate sexual contact or through direct contact with infected blood. They added that scientists were almost certain that saliva did not transmit the virus.

However, one by one the parents of Ari's friends said how sorry they were, but that they could not allow their children to play with her any longer—they were worried that their children might somehow catch the virus from Ari.

"Most of our friends mirrored the vulnerability of the nation," Elizabeth said. "They wanted to stand beside us, but they also wanted assurances that there was absolutely no risk to their children if they continued to play with Ariel and Jake."[6]

Elizabeth recalled, "That year Ari was not invited to any birthday parties. I was devastated, as any mother would be, perhaps even more than Ari."[7] And when the Glasers told Ari's summer camp about her HIV status, they were told that she was no longer welcome. Feeling isolated and alone, Elizabeth and Paul tried to keep up a brave front. But Elizabeth said that she felt as if even strangers could sense that there was something different about her and her family. "Every time I went into the supermarket I envisioned everyone slowly and silently moving away as if they had just seen a rattlesnake."[8]

As September approached, Elizabeth prepared herself to

tell Ari's kindergarten that her daughter was HIV-positive. Ari had been accepted to Crossroads, a private school, and Elizabeth expected they would be told to find another school.

Instead, the school director assured them that Ari would be very welcome at Crossroads and that although they did not have an AIDS policy in place, they would begin drafting one immediately. Elizabeth was so relieved she starting crying.

There was also another reason to celebrate in 1987. The surgeon general announced that saliva did not transmit HIV. Many of Ari's friends were once again allowed to play with her because now their parents could trust that Ari would not transmit the disease to them through normal, everyday childhood activities. Elizabeth felt very grateful that her friends were willing to overcome their fears by learning the facts. She knew that many other families with HIV-infected children were not as fortunate.

By the summer of 1987 Ari was getting weaker. Her T cell count was significantly down. T cells are the white blood cells that defend the immune system. HIV infects T cells and then kills them. The fewer T cells a person has, the more susceptible he or she is to various infections and diseases, such as pneumonia and cancer. People with HIV do not die from having the virus but from secondary infections.

Elizabeth discovered that AZT, the only drug that had been useful in treating AIDS in adults, was not available for children. Her doctor explained that there had not been enough tests completed to determine if AZT was safe for children, but he hoped it would be approved by the fall. This was the first time that Elizabeth came face-to-face with the inadequacy of research being done about pediatric AIDS.

By the start of school in September, Ari was experiencing terrible stomach cramps that made her scream and cry. Nevertheless, she insisted on going to first grade. After the first two weeks, she was too sick to continue and had to remain at home. Her teacher frequently dropped by to help her work on her lessons, and Elizabeth spent every day reading with Ari, painting pictures, and teaching her math. Jake adored his older sister and devised all sorts of games to entertain her.

By Thanksgiving, Ari was in the hospital with an infected pancreas that gave her excruciating chronic pain. In March, Ari contracted pneumonia, and the doctors informed the Glasers that her nervous system was deteriorating and that her brain had started shrinking. She could no longer speak or move. Even AZT, which had finally been approved for children, was doing nothing to help her.

Staring at her dying child, Elizabeth realized that she could no longer stand by quietly. "I have to do something," she thought. "I have to do something to save my child!"[9]

Desperately studying everything she could find about pediatric AIDS, she discovered that the majority of federal funds spent on AIDS research was focused on the impact of AIDS in adults. Frequently, such experiments were not beneficial to children because the disease often took a very different course in young people. It became clear that children were not getting their fair share of federal research dollars. One reason she felt this was allowed to happen was that there was no one lobbying on Capitol Hill for children with AIDS.

Lobbyists encourage members of Congress to vote for funding and other initiatives that help their causes. There are lobbyists in Washington representing a wide range of groups and interests, including people with different types of diseases, such as breast cancer or diabetes.

When Elizabeth realized that there was no one speaking on behalf of children with AIDS, she said, "I felt a mantle of responsibility descend over my shoulders. It was a frightening and unforgettable moment."[10] Immediately, she set up appointments with politicians and government officials.

During one of her conversations with doctors at the National Institute of Health, she discovered that there had been a few studies showing that AZT taken intravenously, rather than in pill form, had helped some children with AIDS. Ari had tried the pills without success, but Elizabeth convinced her doctor to administer the drug intravenously.

After three weeks of this treatment Ari started improving. One day, when Elizabeth went into her bedroom, her daughter sat up and said, "Good morning, Mom. I love you."[11]

Elizabeth recalled, "I couldn't believe it. Ari was back. Maybe miracles did happen. Maybe one was going to happen in our house."[12]

A few days later Ari was well enough to go to the Santa Monica pier and ride the Ferris wheel. Two weeks later, however, her illness grew worse, and she was again admitted to the hospital. A few days after her seventh birthday, Ari died.

"Paul wept," Elizabeth said, "and I cried 'Noooo!' It was a no that wanted to turn back time. It was a no to a world that had failed me."[13]

After Ari's death Elizabeth was more committed than ever to fighting for children with AIDS. She continued putting pressure on congressional leaders to increase funding so that it would be more consistent with that spent on adults with the disease. She also met with President Ronald Reagan and his wife, Nancy, and told them how isolated her family had felt after their HIV diagnosis and urged them to do whatever they could to educate the public about the disease.

All of her hard work paid off when the federal budget for pediatric AIDS research increased from $3.3 million to $8.8 million. Still, this was less money than she felt was needed, and she concluded that "there would be a role for a small foundation that would fill the gap until the government took over its responsibility."[14]

With two friends, she established the Pediatric AIDS Foundation (PAF). Using their connections in Hollywood and Washington, D.C., the PAF soon had an impressive board of directors, including movie director Steven Spielberg and Michael Eisner (the CEO of Walt Disney).

Because the organization was staffed by volunteers who worked out of donated office space without salaries, 90 percent of all the money raised was spent directly on programs to benefit work in pediatric AIDS. Within the first eight months Elizabeth and the PAF acquired $2.2 million to finance forty research grants.

In 1992 Democratic presidential candidate Bill Clinton asked Elizabeth to speak at the Democratic National Convention. She was thrilled. She knew that this was a chance to bring her message to millions of television viewers. She wanted to remind people that children with AIDS are blameless victims who deserve compassion and respect. She wanted to use the story of her own family's tragedy to try to ensure that in the future children with HIV would not be ostracized by their communities or barred from their schools.

On July 14, she stepped onto the stage before 20,000 delegates at Madison Square Garden in New York City. She was terrified, but then "she felt a small hand squeeze hers tightly, and she could clearly see Ariel."[15] She felt certain that her daughter was watching over her. She told the audience that Ari "taught me to love when all I wanted to do was hate; she taught me to help others when all I wanted to do was help myself."[16] Many in the audience were moved to tears.

By 1994 the PAF had raised $30 million for Pediatric AIDS research. In February of that year, scientists announced that a PAF-sponsored program had found ways to use AZT to treat pregnant women to reduce by 60 percent the chance they will pass the virus on to their fetuses.

On December 3, 1994, Elizabeth Glaser died. Jake was still healthy, although one family friend said, "His mother is gone, his sister is gone, and he has the same disease. It is pretty hard to absorb."[17] Today, there is hope for Jake and children like him because doctors are experimenting with combinations of drugs that they hope will eradicate HIV in some patients.

FIVE

❧

DELORES HUERTA

The sun was just beginning to rise when Delores Huerta climbed out of her beat-up old car on a deserted road at the edge of a vineyard. She grabbed a homemade sign that read *Huelga!* (Strike!). She wanted to encourage the men and women toiling in those fields to join thousands of other California farmworkers who were refusing to pick the grapes until the growers agreed to increase wages and provide better working conditions. But as she leaned on her sign, she suddenly saw a car roaring toward her. Just before it was about to hit her, Delores leaped and rolled out of its way.

Throughout her long career as a founding member and chief negotiator for the United Farm Workers, Delores Huerta has had many similar brushes with danger. Nevertheless, she continues to fight for the right of the mainly Latino farmworkers to be protected under the same laws that govern other workers in America, including child labor regulations, minimum wage guarantees, and unemployment benefits.

She has said, "I kind of think of [labor] organizing as sacred work. . . . It's a big responsibility, you know getting peo ple's hopes up, and then if you abandon them . . . well, you've ruined their aspirations, and you've spoiled the faith they have to have in anybody who tries to help them."[1]

Delores Fernandez was born on April 10, 1930, in Dawson, New Mexico. Her father was a mine worker and union activist. After being blacklisted for his activism, he was forced to take a low-paying job as a farmworker in the beet fields of Wyoming and Nebraska. When Delores was six, her parents divorced. In 1942 Delores's mother began running a hotel that rented rooms to migrant farmworkers in Stockton, California. Delores said, "My mother was one of those women who do a lot. She was divorced, so I never really understood what it meant for a woman to take a back seat to a man."[2]

During the week, Delores helped her mother after school doing chores around the hotel. On school vacations, she worked eight-hour days packing apricots. She was paid a few pennies for each tray she filled. Although she worked as fast as she could, she rarely managed to fill more than eight trays a day.

In 1948 Delores married her high school sweetheart, an Irishman. She had the first two of what would eventually be eleven children. By the time she was twenty, she was divorced. Her mother took care of the children while Delores took night classes to earn a teaching credential.

The elementary-age children she taught were mainly from families of farmworkers. Most attended school only sporadically, because they had to help their parents in the fields. Delores said, "I couldn't stand seeing kids come to class hungry and needing shoes. I thought I could do more by organizing the farm workers than by trying to teach . . . hungry children."[3]

In 1955 she began working for Stockton's Community Service Organization (CSO), which had been started by Fred Ross, to help increase political power in Latino communities, including the farmworkers. The CSO led voter registration drives and lobbied for more Latinos on the police force and for Spanish-speaking personnel in hospitals and governmental offices.

Delores's energy seemed limitless. She threw herself into her work and was appointed the CSO's full-time lobbyist at the California state capitol in Sacramento. She also married a man named Ventura Huerta. In her two years as a lobbyist, she was instrumental in pushing through numerous pieces of legislation that included bills extending social insurance coverage to farmworkers and Mexican aliens, increasing welfare benefits, and requiring that the examinations for drivers' licenses be given in Spanish as well as English.

She recognized, however, that legislation alone "could not solve the real problem" of the farmworkers.[4] They needed to be organized in order to effectively demand higher pay and better working conditions.

This was the same conclusion reached by another bright, energetic young Mexican-American CSO worker named Cesar Chavez. He had urged the CSO to begin unionizing the farmworkers but met with resistance. Frustrated, he resigned from his post in March of 1962. He decided he would have to organize the workers himself. Taking what little money he had in his bank account, he moved with his wife and eight children to Delano, California. He asked Delores Huerta to help him establish the Farm Workers Association (FWA).

Chavez and Huerta had initially been introduced to each other by Fred Ross in 1955. Ross had recognized that they were both people "who cannot live with themselves and see injustice in front of them. They must go after it whenever they see it, no matter how much time it takes and no matter how many sleepless nights of worry."[5]

The first six months of 1962 Chavez and Huerta traveled all over California, meeting with workers and asking them to support the FWA. It was hard work. They were asking families that had been poverty-stricken for generations to believe that change was possible through the FWA.

Later in 1962 they decided the time was right to hold a convention in Fresno, California, to officially establish the Farm Workers Association. It was attended by three hundred delegates from around the state. Chavez was elected president and Huerta vice president. They both spoke, and then Cesar's brother, Manuel, unfurled a flag he had designed for the FWA. It had a red background with a white circle and a heroic-looking eagle, like the one in the center of Mexico's flag. Manuel told the workers, "When the eagle flies, the problems of the farm worker will be solved."[6]

For three years Huerta and Chavez worked to bring more members into the FWA, and soon there were enough families paying dues to make the FWA self-supporting. The name of the group was also changed to the National Farm Workers Association (NFWA) to express their hopes that one day it would eventually represent all farmworkers in the United States, not just those in California.

On September 8, 1965, news reached the NFWA headquarters that Filipino farmworkers were on strike because they were getting paid less than workers in other vineyards. The Filipinos had their own union, the American Workers Organizing Committee (AWOC). Chavez and Huerta realized that if AWOC went on strike, then the NFWA would also have to go on strike; otherwise, the growers could use one union against the other. But was the NFWA ready to go on strike?

Huerta and Chavez knew that if they encouraged workers to go on strike, they would have no incomes, and the union, with its small budget, would somehow have to find a way to help provide basic necessities for these people.

Before they made a decision, Delores met with the Filipinos. She discovered that the growers wanted to slash their wages by almost a third, down to one dollar an hour. The growers were throwing the strikers out of shacks they had lived in for years and were patrolling the fields with guns.

At a meeting of the NFWA, Delores told members what she

had learned. As she spoke, she could see the anger on their faces. We must help our fellow workers, she told the crowd. They cannot do it alone. The audience erupted in cheers of support. The NFWA had embarked on its first official strike.

It quickly became clear that the growers were determined to keep the strikers away from their fields and at times resorted to violent tactics to try to scare them off. Strikers were beaten. They had guns fired over their heads. Still, they did not back down. And they did not respond with violence.

This was largely due to Cesar's leadership. He had been strongly influenced by the peaceful civil rights movement led by Martin Luther King, Jr. Delores said, "Having the women and the children out on the picket line [also] made it a lot easier to maintain the nonviolence stance."[7]

Sometimes Delores would bring some of her children to the protests. More often, her long hours and busy traveling schedule meant that she had to leave her children behind in the care of her mother or friends. She said later, "My biggest problem was not to feel guilty about it. . . . Everybody used to lay these guilt trips on me, about what a bad mother I was, neglecting my children. . . . Of course, I had no way of knowing what the effects on my kids would be. Now . . . I can look back and say it's O.K. because my kids turned out fine, even though at times they had to fend for themselves."[8]

As the strike continued, the workers were joined by other supporters including religious leaders, civil rights workers, and college students. But by December 1965, Huerta and Chavez had decided that the strike alone was not going to bring about the necessary changes. The growers were hiring braceros, or Mexican workers. These workers would not know they were going to be strikebreakers until they got to the American fields. The growers knew that even if some of the braceros joined the picket lines, there were always many more impoverished Mexicans willing to replace them.

Huerta and Chavez knew they had to find a way to hit the

growers in their pocketbooks. They decided to announce a boycott, focusing primarily on one particularly large grower.

In February of 1966 the NFWA led a protest march to draw public attention to the boycott. The NFWA members marched from Delano to the state capital of Sacramento, three hundred miles to the north. By the time the marchers reached the capital, the streets were lined with cheering supporters. The growers' executives were ready to negotiate and concede many of the union's demands.

There were many other growers who were still exploiting their workers, but the NFWA found that the mere threat of another boycott brought a number of these companies to the bargaining table. Delores Huerta became the chief negotiator for the contracts signed with the growers. At first, she said, "I had never seen a contract before. I talked to labor people, I got copies of contracts and studied them for a week and a half, so I knew something when I came to the workers."⁹

During this time, the NFWA and the AWOC merged into the United Farm Workers Organizing Committee or UFWOC. Despite their successes, the UFWOC had signed contracts covering only about 5,000 of California's 250,000 farmworkers. The UFWOC decided to attack the biggest grower of table grapes, the Guimarra Corporation. "If we can crack Guimarra," Delores Huerta announced, "we can crack them all."¹⁰

The company immediately stymied the boycott by shipping grapes under 100 different labels. This meant that even if consumers wanted to join the boycott, there was no way they could know if the grapes came from Guimarra fields or not. The UFWOC had to declare a boycott on all table grapes.

In January of 1968 Delores Huerta climbed on an old rusty school bus with sixty other UFWOC members to head to New York City to set up boycotts. This city bought more grapes than any other in the country. "It was the first time we'd done anything like that," she recalled. "There were no ground rules.

I thought, 11 million people in New York, and I have to persuade them to stop buying grapes."[11]

Delores began by meeting with numerous civic, civil rights, and college groups. She helped supporters paint posters and signs announcing "Boycott California Grapes." She had bumper stickers made and held news conferences. She arranged for boycott committees to be set up in other cities across the country.

Soon shipments of grapes were being met by pickets in small towns and big cities all across the country. Demonstrators marched in front of supermarkets and handed out leaflets explaining the boycott. In Boston, supporters dumped shipments of grapes into the harbor in a re-creation of the Boston Tea Party. Soon entire supermarket chains had quit stocking the grapes.

During the summer of 1968, New York's grape sales dropped 90 percent. By the next year, Coachella Valley grape growers lost $3 million in grape sales. By mid-July of 1970 growers were ready to bargain.

Once again, Delores Huerta was in charge of these negotiations. She said that because she was breast-feeding, "they would just have to wait while the baby ate. . . . [It] made the employers sensitive to the fact that when we were talking about benefits in terms of a contract, we were talking about families and we were talking about children."[12]

Contracts were signed with twenty-six growers who produced half of California's entire grape crop. The base pay for workers increased from $1.65 in 1971 to $2.05 in 1972. Growers also agreed to create a union hiring hall where workers could enroll to find employment and to set up worker-grower committees to regulate the use of pesticides. "What's happened here is a miracle," Delores said. "But it didn't come about by magic."[13]

The UFWOC's next target was the workers in Salinas and

Santa Maria valleys who harvested most of the nation's lettuce, strawberries, and some other vegetables. The growers in America's "Salad Bowl" region realized that they could head off the UFWOC's advances by signing with a different union that would make fewer demands on them and at the same time allow them to assure consumers that their workers had union representation.

Many of these growers signed with the Teamsters Union, which primarily represented truckers. The Teamsters were happy to have more members paying dues and giving them more influence. Chavez called this "an act of treason against the legitimate aspirations of farm workers" and declared "all-out war . . . against the Teamsters and the bosses."[14]

A national lettuce boycott was called. The Teamsters responded by going after UFWOC grape contracts in 1973 and winning most of them. This sparked violent farm-labor strife; two UFWOC members were killed, and more than 3,500 were arrested for violating injunctions against picketing and demonstrations. Worried about the violence, Chavez and Huerta called off all picketing and focused on a boycott not only of lettuce but also of grapes from Teamster-controlled fields.

Huerta and Chavez also decided to call a convention of their members to reaffirm the goals of the UFWOC. Four hundred delegates attended, and Delores helped preside over the final session. The UFWOC decided that it would charge members dues only when working, set up a peer review board to handle complaints against the union, and recommitted itself to not using violence to settle disagreements.

In 1975 Chavez and Huerta decided to hold another march to protest the low wages and poor working conditions of field workers for the Gallo wineries. Nearly 15,000 people marched past the wineries, the largest demonstration ever for the UFWOC. This protest eventually led Governor Edmund Brown to establish an Agricultural Labor Relations Board to hear unfair labor practice charges and to conduct union elections. Delores was thrilled. This board helped give workers the right to join the union of their choice and to take control of their economic futures. Four months later, Brown signed another bill giving unemployment insurance to farmworkers.

By the fall of 1975 growers were becoming desperate. Seventeen million people had stopped buying grapes and fourteen million had stopped buying lettuce.[15] The UFWOC forced the growers to hold union elections immediately rather than waiting for the new law to go into effect.

The UFWOC managed to sign new contracts with 165 lettuce growers and to raise the workers' base pay by an impressive 16 percent. However, in other elections, farmworkers were being coerced into voting for growers' candidates. Also, the Agricultural Labor Relations Board was clogged with complaints. These problems persisted throughout the 1980s, and Delores Huerta continued to work to address them.

In 1988 she and other UFWOC supporters held a rally outside the West St. Francis Hotel in San Francisco to protest Vice President George Bush's opposition to the ongoing grape boycott. The police advanced with their batons to clear the road. Huerta suffered six broken ribs and a ruptured spleen. The scene was videotaped by a bystander, and in September 1989 Huerta and six other protesters sued the city, stating their civil rights had been violated. She was awarded $825,000 in what would be one of San Francisco's largest police misconduct settlements ever. Her lawyer stated, "Change was one thing Delores insisted upon. As a result, the city issued a whole new manual on crowd control techniques."[16]

Delores Huerta has won many awards for her tireless crusade. She has been inducted into the Women's Hall of Fame and in 1993 won the NAACP Martin Luther King, Jr., Award. She continues to work as the union's vice president and knows that there will be many battles in the future. But she says, "When you need people, they come to you. You find a way. . . . It gets easier all the time."[17]

SIX

〰

PATRICIA
IRELAND

In December of 1991 Patricia Ireland was elected the ninth president of the 280,000-member National Organization of Women (NOW), the largest and most prominent feminist group in America. NOW was founded in 1966 by a group of feminist leaders, and its objective is to support abortion rights and to fight sexual discrimination in education and employment.

In the past three decades, women have made tremendous strides in their struggle for equality. Women have moved into the workforce in large numbers and joined previously male-dominated professions; they have won equal access to sports, higher education, and credit.

Despite these successes, Patricia Ireland does not believe that the fight for sexual equality has ended. She said that in the past "we realized that the gains we had made were not irreversible. We must bear in mind . . . that the progress we seek [today] is not inevitable. It will come because we have new energy in our movement."[1]

〰

Patricia Ireland was born on October 19, 1945, in Oak Park, Illinois. Her father was a metallurgical engineer for a company that would become the largest magnet manufacturer in the world. Her mother worked at a tailor's shop, but after giving birth to Patricia's older sister, Kathy, she never worked outside the house again.

Patricia recalled that although "the role of 1950's wife and mother seemed to suit her to a tee . . ., the message my mother inadvertently gave me throughout childhood and adolescence was not to comply with authority, but to challenge it."[2]

When Patricia was four and a half years old, her older sister died in a horseback riding accident. Patricia's parents decided to adopt two little girls to try to help ease their grief, but Patricia said that her father "never, never got over it."[3] Throughout her childhood, Patricia tried to make up for her parents' loss by being the perfect daughter. In high school she was on the honor roll and the pep squad.

She said, "I never envisioned anything but a conventional . . . future for myself. I would go on to college. But after that, like my mother before me, I'd get a job for a while, then marry and have children. I would stay at home to raise them and live happily ever after."[4]

At the age of sixteen she went to DePauw University in Greencastle, Indiana. After her first year she married her boyfriend, Donald Anderson. He was a year older than Patricia and had been attending Ball State University. After the wedding, the young couple transferred to the University of Tennessee together. A year later, however, the marriage had dissolved and they divorced.

In 1966 Patricia graduated with a degree in German. At the time, most college-educated women could choose between three traditionally acceptable professions—teaching, nursing, and secretarial work. After an unhappy year of teaching, she said that none of the other careers appealed to her. "The only thing that chilled me more than the sight of other people's bodily fluids was the sight of a typewriter," she joked.[5]

In 1967 she decided to move to Miami to become a flight attendant for an airline company. She looked forward to traveling all over the world, but was also aware that the airline industry was one "that actually seemed to *invite* sexual harassment [of flight attendants] with such ads as 'We really move our tails for you' or 'I'm Cheryl: Fly me.'"[6]

During training sessions, she found that the airline had very strict rules about the appearance of female flight attendants. They had to be thin and wear their hair in certain styles. They also had to wear pumps that were at least three inches high and a girdle.

All flight attendants were drilled to be polite to passengers, no matter how rude or surly they might be, and deferential to the male flight crew. Such training, the airline assured them, would be excellent preparation for marriage. Patricia became increasingly frustrated by these regulations. She felt that it was demeaning to have to say "Thank you, thank you," as she collected the passengers' garbage, and she resented the expectation that she would brush off sexual propositions with nothing more than a smile and a laugh.

She recalled that the turning point came for her when a plane she was working on received a bomb threat and was evacuated. The pilot asked her to stay on board and cook him a steak. She said, "I had resigned myself to the other hazards of a lowly flight attendant's role: the long hours, low pay, leering passengers, groping copilots. But in that moment I realized that I had no real obligation to lay my own life on the line for our captain's dinner."[7] She left the plane and told him to cook his own dinner.

"Consciousness," she said, "is a funny thing. Once you become conscious, you can't just regress. You find yourself becoming conscious of more and more."[8] She began reading feminist books and learning more about the increasingly powerful feminist movement.

During her first year at the airline company, Patricia decided to challenge one of its discriminatory policies. In 1968 she had married her second husband, an artist, named James Humble. When he needed his wisdom teeth pulled, Patricia expected that he would be covered under her health insurance plan. She was informed by the airline that although wives were covered by the plan, husbands were not. If she had been a man, she would have gotten coverage for her family, but as woman she was not entitled to it.

She decided to telephone the local chapter of NOW for advice. They advised her of her legal rights and helped her force the airline to back down and change its policy. Patricia said that this experience was life-altering. "Not only did I learn how much power a movement has, but even my saying 'This isn't right' and getting mad was enough to make a good thing happen for other women."[9] After this, she started volunteering for the Dade County NOW and becoming more involved with the feminist movement. She also decided to become a lawyer.

She enrolled at Florida State University Law School in 1972 and later transferred to the University of Miami. On the weekends and holidays she continued to work for the airline to pay her tuition. She found that people would treat her differently depending on whether she told them she was a law student or a flight attendant. The former gave her instant credibility, while the latter led many to discount her ideas. She considered this an infuriating example of how jobs that have been traditionally held by women in our society—like that of flight attendant—are often undervalued and that the women who hold these jobs are denigrated. On the other hand, careers that have been traditionally male dominated— like the law—carry with them prestige and status.

64

It was not surprising to her that law school, which for many years had been the exclusive domain of men, was tainted by sexism. At times male lecturers would make derogatory remarks about women, and one of her property law textbooks included the sentence "Land, like a woman, was meant to be possessed."[10] This phrase was struck from later editions of the book after Patricia wrote an angry letter to the publisher.

After graduating with high honors in 1975, Patricia joined a corporate law firm. Her plan was to one day run for elected office, and she said that "with the money and influence I hoped to access as a lawyer, I'd be able to tap the necessary financial resources and personal connections . . . to get elected."[11] In her free time, she helped corporate companies establish affirmative action programs that promoted women and minorities, and she continued to volunteer for NOW.

At the time, NOW was focusing much of its energy on the fight for the passage of the Equal Rights Amendment (ERA). This proposed constitutional amendment stated: "Equality of rights under the law shall not be denied or abridged by the United States or by any State on account of sex."

The ERA was originally proposed in 1923, soon after women won the vote. But for many years it had been bottled up in committees, until 1971 when the House and Senate passed the amendment and sent it on to the states for ratification. Three fourths of all the states would have to vote in favor of the ERA in order for it to become law. Congress had imposed an arbitrary seven-year deadline in which the amendment had to be ratified.

Patricia felt the ERA was necessary because a number of states still had sexually discriminatory laws that gave preference to men over women in employment and that recognized the man in the family as the sole "head and master" of the household. Among other things, these so-called head and master laws gave men the right to mortgage the family house over their wives' objections and the right to control their wives' earnings.

Such laws had a strong impact on women's lives. For instance, Patricia recalled that in Dade County, Florida, "Women constituted nearly a third of all Metro Dade employees at the time, but more than 90 percent of the jobs paying twenty-five thousand dollars or more per year went to men. . . . The federal work incentive program was mandated *by law* to give priority for job training and placement to unemployed fathers [over unemployed mothers]."[12]

In October of 1978 Congress extended the deadline for ratification of the ERA until June 30, 1982. In 1980 Patricia led demonstrations against Florida's elected representatives who were in opposition to the amendment. She was also working as the pro bono (unpaid) legal counsel for the Dade County NOW, taking on numerous antidiscrimination cases and advising women of their rights.

It became increasingly clear that there were not enough votes for the ERA to pass. Nevertheless, NOW continued lobbying on behalf of the bill. "We had to go on," Patricia said, "otherwise, our opposition would smell blood and that would make them too eager to take us on in future battles."[13] Further, she felt that the fight for the ERA was helping to build new coalitions and strengthening networks. For the first time since women demanded the right to vote, large numbers of women were banding together around a single issue.

When in 1982 the ERA failed to be ratified, Patricia Ireland was not completely discouraged. She said that the battle had "focused the attention of the entire nation on the extent of discrimination against women and on what equality . . . could mean. . . . We raised the country's consciousness."[14]

In 1985 Patricia Ireland was picked to manage Eleanor Smeal's successful bid for NOW's presidency. Two years later Patricia was offered a paid officer position as NOW's treasurer. She made the difficult decision to leave Florida and her job in corporate law to move to the organization's national action center in Washington, D.C. Her husband, James, remained behind in Florida.

Six weeks after she arrived at the nation's capital, President Eleanor Smeal called her into her office to tell her that she was not planning on running for another term. She hoped that Patricia would run in her place. At the time, Patricia did not feel ready to take over the leadership of the organization. However, she did agree to run as the executive vice president on a successful ticket headed by the firebrand and grandmother Molly Yard.

During Patricia's vice presidency, NOW was primarily focused on the struggle about abortion rights. During the Republican pro-life administrations of Presidents Reagan and Bush, there had been an increase in the militant activism of pro-life groups like Operation Rescue. In response, Patricia Ireland organized NOW's Project Stand Up for Women. This program was based on a three-pronged strategy that called for the use of lawsuits to restrict the actions of protesters blocking women's access to the clinics, an array of nonviolent responses to keep the clinics open, and an increase in the political pressure put on public officials to encourage them to support the pro-choice movement. During her vice presidency, Patricia also organized conferences, led marches, and represented NOW at international conferences.

In 1990 she ran for reelection on a successful ticket with Molly Yard. In April of 1991, Molly Yard suffered a massive stroke and had to step down from office. Patricia Ireland took over the role of president. Soon after, she made headlines by acknowledging that she now had a female partner. Many in the organization had assumed that she was heterosexual and felt that her revelation would support the stereotype that all feminists are lesbians. Patricia was unapologetic, stating, "This is how I live my life and I'm not ashamed."[15]

Her first public action as NOW president was to lead a

massive march that protested President George Bush's nomination of Clarence Thomas as a Supreme Court justice. A former colleague of Thomas's, Anita Hill, had testified before a congressional committee that he had sexually harassed her. Despite these accusations, the all-male congressional committee approved Thomas's appointment to the bench. Ironically, this event proved to be a watershed moment for feminists because it focused the national spotlight on sexual harassment, a problem that many women (including Patricia Ireland) had encountered in the workforce. It also highlighted the necessity of having more female representatives on Capitol Hill. In 1992 a record number of women were elected to Congress in what would become known as the "Year of the Woman."

The Thomas hearings also led to an upsurge in NOW's membership. People were signing up at three times the usual rate. "The irony is that the women's movement prospers in adversity," Patricia said. "When things get bad we get more supporters, more activists, more money, more everything."[16]

One of the first steps Patricia took after assuming office was to define the role NOW would take in advocating women's rights in Washington. In 1985 a NOW president had been ousted after she met with 1984 Democratic presidential candidate Walter Mondale and persuaded him to pick Geraldine Ferraro as his vice presidential running mate. Ireland stated that she had no intention of allowing the organization to become another inside-the-beltway lobbying group, taking congressional leaders out to lunch, and "begging men for our rights."[17] "Our role," she has said, "is to be at the cutting edge of controversy."[18]

Some of the plans she outlined for the future included the establishment of a television network that would be devoted to feminist issues. It would present, among other things, a segment in which women would describe abuse and discrimination by employers, and viewers would be encouraged to boycott these employers' products.

Patricia Ireland also stated that she hoped to develop training sessions for NOW activists that would prepare them to perform various acts of nonviolence to draw attention to their concerns. For instance, she envisioned a demonstration in which women would lay a wreath on the steps of the Supreme Court in memory of women who had died from illegal abortions.

She has also stated that in the future she would like to take a leadership role in organizing a new political party to pressure both Democrats and Republicans to become more feminist.

In 1993 Patricia Ireland ran for reelection against South Carolina attorney Efia Nwangaza. Nwangaza, who is black, charged that NOW was an elitist organization of mainly middle-class white women. She disputed Ireland's assertion that NOW welcomed diversity and had always been committed to addressing the concerns of lower-income women and women of color.

"The appearance of diversity is not enough," Nwangaza stated, adding that minority women held only token positions in the organization's national leadership.[19] After a contentious campaign, Ireland won by a sizable margin, although Nwangaza managed to win a quarter of the votes cast and did not rule out another run for the presidency in the future.

That same year the organization won a major victory in the abortion rights struggle. Earlier Patricia had helped NOW devise a strategy that would use the Racketeer Influenced and Corrupt Organizations Act (RICO) against pro-life protesters who blocked access to clinics. RICO was originally enacted in 1970 to prosecute members of organized crime. It bans "any person employed or associated with any enterprise . . . to participate in a pattern of racketeering activity," including extortion.[20] Patricia reasoned that NOW could use RICO to charge antiabortion groups with extortion through their use of arson, bombings, destruction of property, assault and battery, trespass, and harassment at clinics. In May 1993 the Supreme Court unanimously voted to allow NOW to use RICO to sue antiabortion groups blocking clinics.

In 1994 Patricia Ireland and NOW focused their attention on trying to stop budget cuts proposed by a newly elected right-wing Congress led by Newt Gingrich. Patricia called their plan to cut social programs an attempt "to rip away the safety net for women and children in order to line the pockets of corporations."[21] In April 1995 she organized a massive rally in Washington, D.C., that was endorsed by more than seven hundred groups and fifty members of Congress.

In August 1995 after the annual NOW conference, Patricia Ireland announced that members had voted to start pushing for a new ERA. This amendment would be broader in scope than the original one. It would affirm a woman's right to an abortion and specify that "all persons shall have equal rights and privileges without discrimination on account of sex, race, sexual orientation, marital status, ethnicity, national origin, color or indigence."[22] Later, age and disability were added as protected categories as well.

Working long hours, Patricia Ireland continues to play many different roles as the leader of NOW. On one day in 1996 she could be found in Illinois standing outside a car manufacturing plant with a picket sign, supporting women workers who had filed a sexual harassment suit against the company. On another day she would be in Long Beach, California, leading a rally against an initiative that would end affirmative action. In the course of a single afternoon she might go from leading a protest to meeting with congressional leaders. She has said, "I want it all. I want to do everything. I don't see why I can't have my cake and eat it too."[23]

She hopes to remain in office through the year 2000 and to keep pushing for changes to make America a more just society for all people. She knows that she will make enemies along the way because sometimes, as she has said, "taking a leadership position makes people uncomfortable. But my ultimate value isn't comfort. My ultimate value is progress for women."[24]

SEVEN

⟡

Maggie
Kuhn

With her white bun and granny glasses, Maggie Kuhn looked like a storybook little old lady. But instead of handing out cookies and milk, she barnstormed around the country, gave speeches, and met with powerful politicians. Angered by the prejudices and discrimination she encountered as an old person, she founded a group in 1970 that would become known as the Gray Panthers. They were dedicated to eradicating ageism (discrimination against people who are old) and bringing "young and old together for a better world for the young to grow old in."[1] By 1988 the Gray Panthers had 60,000 members nationwide.

Maggie Kuhn believed that students and retired people were natural allies, sharing many of the same concerns as well as obstacles to empowerment. Further, she felt that both groups had the freedom and inclination to be more radical than most adults in the workforce, who were focused on saving money, raising families, and planning for the future.

She said that both old and young people are "out of the [political] mainstream, and they're not taken seriously. People in power positions think that the old don't know much because we don't do much. And they think of children as not having very much to say because, well, they're children. . . . Yet both are free to be the change agents, to change society, to work for an enduring peace."[2]

Maggie Kuhn was born on August 3, 1905, into a family of socially conscious activists. Her aunt had been a passionate suffragist, and one of her grandparents helped smuggle fugitive slaves to Canada via the Underground Railroad. Her mother, Minnie Louise Kuhn, was shunned by neighbors in Memphis, Tennessee, when they discovered that she invited her black cleaning woman to sit down at the table with her for lunch. When she was pregnant with Maggie she left Memphis to travel north to Buffalo, New York, because she did not want her daughter born in the segregated South. A few weeks later she returned to Memphis with the child. Three years later she gave birth to Maggie's sickly younger brother, Sam.

Maggie's father, Samuel Kuhn, was a businessman for a company that would eventually become the well-known and prosperous firm of Dun and Bradstreet. He was frequently transferred, and the family moved from Memphis to Louisville, Kentucky, and then to Cleveland, Ohio.

Maggie recalled, "My father believed that everyone could achieve success no matter how deprived their beginnings."[3] The key to success, her father felt, was to set goals, work hard, and be virtuous. Religion was very important to the family, and Maggie's father was one of the lay leaders of the Presbyterian Church.

In 1922, at the age of sixteen, Maggie graduated from West High School and went on to the College for Women at Western Reserve University, where she was an honor student majoring in English with minors in sociology and French. She recalled that at the time women "were given two career options—nursing and teaching—and it was expected that any career would be interrupted early on for marriage."[4]

In her senior year Maggie decided that she wanted to be a teacher and began working as a teacher's aide at a local junior high school. One day the teacher left her alone in a classroom of ninth graders. Maggie decided to try a creative approach to the grammar lesson and devised a relay race. The students were thrilled until a fight broke out. Many students joined in the tussle, and when the teacher returned, the class was in chaos. After that, Maggie concluded that the chances of her becoming a good teacher were slim.

In 1926, after graduating from college and returning to live in her parents' home, Maggie took a job with Cleveland's Young Women's Christian Association (YWCA). At the time, the Y was a very important organization for young working women. It provided cheap meals, inexpensive rooms, educational programs, and social activities. Programs were implemented to help women deal with the stress of the workplace, organize for better working conditions, and learn new skills so that they could rise to better-paying positions. The Y was one of the few organizations that also allowed women employees to assume executive administrative roles.

In 1930 Maggie's father was transferred to Philadelphia, Pennsylvania, and Maggie moved with the family, taking a job at the Germantown YWCA. She was in charge of programs for business and professional women—mainly secretaries, store clerks, bookkeepers, and elementary school teachers. Maggie wanted the women to realize that collectively they could have power and encouraged them to join unions. She established Sunday night discussion groups where women could discuss important issues of the day and get the intellectual stimulation many were missing at work.

"One of the things I valued most about the Y," Maggie said, "was its belief in the ability of groups to empower the individual and to change society."[5]

In 1941, as the United States was about to enter World War II, Maggie was invited by the National Board of the YWCA to work at the headquarters in New York City. She became an editor for YWCA publications and ran a group that helped the thousands of young women working in the defense industry. Many of them had come from the countryside to take jobs in factories in the cities and quickly found that there was no place for them to live. Through the Y, Maggie helped to arrange for housing, child care, and other forms of support.

In 1948 Maggie took a job with the Unitarian Church in Boston. She later moved to the church's offices in Philadelphia. She began working for the Social Education and Action Department, which was responsible for analyzing important social issues and lobbying for them on the church's behalf. She and her colleagues urged church members to speak out on such issues as racism and nuclear arms.

During these years Maggie also helped publish a magazine called *Social Progress*. Researching articles, Maggie said, "I was always reading up on the latest figures on housing or employment or crime."[6] Spurred on by the problems she was reading about, she and a few of her colleagues started holding meetings with local church groups to help them devise ways to make their own communities better.

In 1965 Maggie was transferred to work in the church's main administrative offices in New York City. She did not want to sell her house and so commuted from Philadelphia to New York every day. In New York, she became the program executive for the Council on Church and Race. In 1972 her book *Get Out There and Do Something About Injustice* was published.

Through her work in the church and its ministries, she was becoming more and more conscious of not only the injustice of racism and sexism but also the discrimination and problems facing the aged.

In 1969 there were twenty million people sixty-five years old or older in the United States and nearly one fourth were living below the poverty line. Many of these poor were women. This poverty among older Americans was due in part to the high cost of medical care, as well as the insufficiency of many people's pensions to meet the costs of living. In 1977 she wrote her book *Maggie Kuhn on Aging*, a record of her dialogue with a group of pastoral students during the mid-1970s. In the book, she urges the students to help "launch a massive attack on ageism in all its oppressive and constraining forms."[7]

She herself had fallen victim to an ageist policy of the church. In 1970 she turned sixty-five, which was the church's mandatory retirement age. Even though she felt able to continue working, she was told that she had to leave her job.

At first she raged, then she cried, then she decided to organize. In 1970 she met with five other professional women who were also facing mandatory retirement. They all felt that despite their age they still had plenty of energy, and resented the assumption that just because they had turned sixty-five they were ready to drop out of public life.

They decided to hold a meeting with other old people who wanted to continue playing an active role in society. They put up signs that read, "Older persons in our society constitute a great national resource which has largely been unrecognized, undervalued, and unused. The purpose of our meeting is to consider how retirees can be involved in new and really significant ways. There should be no limit to our thinking."[8]

Over one hundred people attended the meeting. They unanimously agreed that a prime concern was the Vietnam War. Most wanted to take an active stand against continuing American involvement in the war. Maggie Kuhn realized that this militancy could serve as a natural bridge between the old people and the radical student protesters. Meetings were held in other cities, and it became clear that old people shared concerns with younger people not only about the war but also about problems of social injustice, including racial and sexual discrimination. Further, it was clear that the voices of both young and old people had been ignored too often by those in power. From these meetings the Consultation of Older and Younger Adults for Social Change was born.

In 1971 the Nixon administration was planning the Second White House Conference on Aging to develop policies for older Americans. Most of the participants in this meeting were doctors and social service providers, but only a few were from the ranks of old people themselves. There were no representatives of elderly nonwhites and the elderly poor.

In response, Maggie Kuhn and a black social worker named Hobart Jackson organized a separate conference called the "Black House Conference on Aging." The Consultation of Older and Younger Adults for Social Change also helped stage a protest at the White House. Maggie got a press pass and handed out information to journalists about the problems facing black and poor elderly people.

Following these actions, a television reporter dubbed the group "the Gray Panthers" after the militant civil rights group the Black Panthers. The name appealed to Maggie, although some members of the Consultation thought it suggested erroneously that they were violent like the Black Panthers. After much debate, the name the Gray Panthers was adopted. Maggie said, "We wanted to show we were taking a stand—rocking the system—not just giving lip service."[9]

The Gray Panthers, she vowed, would also be distinguished from other advocacy groups for older people that too often pitted the interests of the old against those of the young. Maggie Kuhn felt that those groups "want to say to the government, you should gimme this or gimme that just because I'm over 65. We don't buy that. What we do suggest is that this nation has plenty of resources to care for its disadvantaged, young, old and its handicapped, without pitting these groups against each other."[10]

Maggie felt it was important to enlist the help of young people in the Gray Panthers, and many high school students worked at the office as volunteers. She said, "It made me realize how seldom high school students are given responsibility and a job to do. They were thrilled that we took them seriously."[11]

As news of the Gray Panthers spread, Maggie Kuhn was interviewed by numerous newspapers and on television programs. By 1973 the Gray Panthers had opened eleven chapters in cities across the country. Consumer activist Ralph Nader gave $25,000 to the organization. On December 1, 1973, his own group, the Retired Professional Action Group, was merged with the Panthers.

Together they compiled an investigative report of the hearing aid industry. As part of the study, five Gray Panther members who had been diagnosed by doctors as having normal hearing went to hearing aid salespeople. They were all prescribed hearing aids. The report made headlines across the country and resulted in new federal regulations on the hearing aid industry.

By 1974 Maggie Kuhn had expanded the Panthers to include groups in most major cities as well as in many smaller ones. They worked on issues ranging from innovations in public transportation for the elderly and disabled to nursing home reform.

Shortly after forming the Gray Panthers, Maggie Kuhn had begun studying nursing homes around the country. She discovered that in most cases, residents were not allowed to participate on the boards and had no say in the running of the homes. Residents routinely complained of boredom, poor food, and a shortage of nurses.

To try to address these problems, she and the Gray Panthers established the National Coalition for Nursing Home Reform. She recalled that when the coalition went into a Philadelphia nursing home to try to form a patients' rights committee, the administrator of the home was "unable to understand that we were taking their patients seriously, [and] asked that our first project be to help the residents make Easter baskets."[12]

In 1973 the Panthers began a three-year study of the industry, which resulted in the book *Nursing Homes: A Citizens' Action Guide*, published in 1977. The Coalition was instrumental in later passing the 1987 Nursing Home Reform Law, which ensured that the status of all nursing home residents is reviewed regularly and that their rights are not violated.

The Gray Panthers also became a watchdog of the media. Maggie realized that too often old people are stereotyped as childlike, helpless, and useless. One Gray Panther study of television programs of 1969 and 1971 found that less than 5 percent of the characters in prime-time dramas were old and that when old people did appear on TV, they were usually either villains or victims. Commenting on a popular comedy of the 1970s, Maggie said, "On nearly every show, a character comes onstage drooling, senile, and slack jawed. Some older people do lose control of their mouth muscles; it's irreversible and it's not funny."[13]

The Gray Panthers established a Media Watch group to target programs that were degrading to old people and brought their protests to television executives and the National Association of Broadcasters Code Board. They forced the industry to include age along with sex and race as sensitive areas that come under the guidelines of the Television Code of Ethics. In September 1977 Maggie testified about the industry's negative stereotyping of the elderly before the Congressional House Select Committee on Aging.

The Gray Panthers not only took on the entertainment industry but also the American Medical Association (AMA).

Maggie wanted to take the excessive profits out of medicine and staged protests and presented papers at AMA meetings. Her vision of health care in the future was one that would be similar to that offered in Canada. All Americans, she hoped, would one day receive automatic universal coverage from "pre-natal care right up through rigor mortis."[14]

By 1988 the Gray Panthers had almost 60,000 members with ninety local networks in twenty-four states. They helped train retired people throughout the country to monitor banks, insurance companies, the courts, and municipal agencies such as zoning boards and planning commissions to make certain that these institutions were meeting the needs of old people.

Maggie's spacious house provided office space for the Gray Panthers. Never having married, she also had always wanted to share her home with others and rented out rooms to younger people. These boarders became like an extended family. "I loved them dearly," she recalled of one young couple. "On Saturday night we would all stay up late watching *Saturday Night Live*, laughing and eating popcorn."[15]

Recognizing that similar arrangements might be a good solution for other old people, she established the National Shared Housing Resource Center in 1981. Currently, four hundred programs exist pairing young people who need cheap housing with older people who have extra rooms to rent. In exchange for low rents, the young people usually offer assistance in housecleaning, errand-running, and other tasks.

Despite her failing health and two battles with cancer, Maggie Kuhn continued to work hard for the Panthers and to travel extensively in the 1990s. On April 22, 1995, she died in the arms of a longtime friend. Just two weeks earlier, she'd been supporting striking transit workers. In her autobiography, she said that she would like her gravestone inscribed with the words "Here lies Maggie Kuhn under the only stone she left unturned."[16]

EIGHT

WILMA MANKILLER

In December 1985 Wilma Mankiller was sworn in as the first woman chief of the Cherokee Nation. She became the leader of a worldwide population of more than 140,000 and controlled an annual budget of more than $75 million. She said, "I was raised in a household where no one ever said to me, 'You can't do this because you're a woman, Indian, or poor.' No one told me there were limitations. Of course, I would not have listened to them if they had tried."[1]

Wilma Mankiller was born on November 18, 1945, in Tahlequah (TAL-uh-kwaw), Oklahoma. She was the sixth of eleven children. Her father, Charley Mankiller, was a full-blooded Cherokee Indian and her mother was Dutch-Irish. The large family lived in a small house on land her father had inherited known as Mankiller Flats. The soil was not good, but they managed to grow most of the food that they needed.

Although they were poor, Wilma was happy at Mankiller

Flats. Her father instilled in all of his children a love for their Indian heritage and would tell them true stories about the history of the Cherokee people. Many of these stories described the injustices the United States government had inflicted upon their ancestors.

For more than one thousand years before white Europeans arrived in America, the Cherokees had lived in the lush land that later became the states of Tennessee, Virginia, West Virginia, South Carolina, Kentucky, Georgia, Alabama, and North Carolina. However, after the Europeans arrived, the Cherokees began to adopt some of the settlers' customs. The men quit hunting and began farming instead. They built schools and learned to read and write in English as well as Cherokee.

As the United States government began to push the Indians to sign more and more treaties giving away parts of their land, the tribes decided it would be advantageous for them to establish a stronger unified government for such negotiations. They elected a chief, an assistant chief, and other leaders who would be in charge of governing what became known as the Cherokee Nation.

In 1828 gold was discovered on Cherokee land, and two years later the Indian Removal Act was passed. This law gave the U.S. government the authority to buy up all of the Indian land east of the Mississippi River. In return, the Indians would be given land in what would become the state of Oklahoma.

Most of the Cherokees refused to give up their land, and in 1838 President Andrew Jackson sent in troops to forcibly move the Cherokees. The soldiers stormed through the villages, ordering people to leave their half-finished meals, to wake children from their naps, to grab whatever possessions they could, and start marching immediately. The Cherokees marched for 1,200 miles through the bitter cold. Four thousand men, women, and children died from disease and exposure on this exodus, which became known as the "Trail of Tears."

The United States government had promised the Indians that on their new land they would be left alone to govern themselves. However, the government went back on its promise, gradually stripping the Indians of the right to self-governance. Finally, in 1934 it passed the Indian Reorganization Act, which replaced tribal government with rules and laws dictated by a federal agency called the Bureau of Indian Affairs (BIA). After this, the Cherokees, like all other Native American tribes, became dependent upon the U.S. government for schooling, health care, housing, and most other social programs.

In the 1950s the U.S. government determined that Indians should be more fully integrated into society, and the BIA began a program known as "termination." Indians were encouraged to leave their homes on reservations and in Indian communities and move to cities with the promise of better jobs and an end to rural poverty. Wilma said, "They tried to mainstream us, to try to take us away from the tribal landbase and the tribal culture."[2]

Wilma's family was one of the many that the BIA relocated to a city. They left for San Francisco in 1956 after a terrible drought devastated the fields of Mankiller Flats. Wilma recalled that her family was startled by "the mysteries of television, indoor plumbing, neon lights, and elevators."[3]

They quickly realized the that BIA's promises of a rosy future in the city were empty. The only job Charley could find was working in a rope factory. Wilma's oldest brother joined their father to try to help make ends meet.

On her first day at school, Wilma was hurt and angered when the teacher read her last name out loud and all the children in her classroom laughed. Back in Oklahoma, "Mankiller" was not considered an unusual name at all. She was also teased about her clothes and her Oklahoma accent.

Wilma felt shy and self-conscious. When she was twelve, she went to live with her grandmother on a farm in Riverbank, Oklahoma. She felt more comfortable surrounded by open land and animals.

At the end of that year, Wilma returned to San Francisco. Her family had moved into the gang-ridden neighborhood of Hunter's Point. Wilma recalled that it was like "a 'no-man's-land' that was constantly under siege."[4] She began to take refuge at the local Indian Center. There she could meet with other young people from similar backgrounds.

In 1963 Wilma graduated from high school. Because school had been such a difficult experience, she had no interest in going on to college. Instead, she moved into her sister's apartment and took a job as a clerical worker for a finance company.

Soon after, she met a handsome Ecuadoran named Hector Hugo Olaya de Bardi. Six months later, they were married. In January 1964 Wilma gave birth to their daughter, Felicia. Two years later, she gave birth to their second girl, Gina.

At first Wilma was content to stay at home and take care of her children, but gradually she began to realize that she wanted more from life. At this time San Francisco was a hotbed of social activism and change. Young people were protesting the Vietnam War and going on civil rights marches. Women were gathering together, examining the role of sexism in their lives, and demanding equality.

Wilma knew that a college education was the surest way to take control of her own destiny. Enrolling first at Skyline Junior College, she later transferred to San Francisco State College. As she began to become more self-confident and involved in the university life, her marriage to Hugo began to dissolve. She recalled, "I wanted to set my own limits and control my destiny. I began to have dreams about more freedom and independence, and I finally came to understand that I did not have to live a life based on someone else's dreams."[5]

At this time the Indian rights movement was becoming more militant and visible. On November 9, 1969, a group of Native Americans, mostly local students, arrived on Alcatraz Island in San Francisco Bay, announcing that they were officially laying claim to the island. At one time the island had been used by the Ohlones, a local Indian tribe. In the 1700s they were driven away by the Spaniards, and after that the island had been the property of the United States government. A federal penitentiary had been built on Alcatraz, but in 1963 the prison was shut down. Indian groups asked that the island now be returned to their community. Their request was denied.

For nineteen months protesters camped on the island. The demonstration was so dramatic, it made headlines in newspapers all across the country. During these months, Wilma Mankiller worked to raise funds and provide goods needed by the protesters.

In May 1971 the activists abandoned Alcatraz. But by then Wilma knew that she wanted to devote herself to helping Indian people. Against the wishes of her husband, she bought a little car and for the next five years traveled all over California meeting with members of various tribes, offering them whatever assistance she could. For example, she worked with the Pit River Tribe in its battle over tribal lands with a utilities company. She also set up a Native American Youth Center in East Oakland and initiated numerous youth programs.

By 1974 it was clear that her marriage was over, and she and Hugo were divorced. Three years later, she decided to return to Tahlequah, Oklahoma, "just to raise my kids and build a house on my land."6 She persuaded the Cherokee Nation to hire her as an economic stimulus coordinator.

Three years earlier, President Richard Nixon had enacted a self-determination policy allowing the Cherokees and other Native tribes to once again establish their own governments and elect their own officials. When Wilma arrived in Oklahoma, Ross Swimmer had been elected tribal chief. He was trying to revitalize Cherokee communities.

In the late 1960s three quarters of all Native Americans were living in poverty, and more than 40 percent were unemployed. Almost one out of every two Native American youths dropped out of high school. The health of the population had deteriorated so severely that the average Indian died while in his or her forties, while the average non-Indian American lived to age seventy.[7]

Ross Swimmer and Wilma Mankiller were a good match. They were both determined to bring hope, prosperity, and health to the Cherokee Nation. Wilma's job was to encourage Indians to enter university programs in environmental and health sciences so that they could bring their training back to their communities. She spent many hours visiting rural villages, talking with their young people, learning what they needed in order to be able to apply and enter college programs, and then finding ways to help them. During this time, she was also working to earn her own bachelor's degree in science and taking graduate courses in community planning at the University of Arkansas.

In 1979 she was promoted to program-development specialist. She felt happy and fulfilled by her life. Then on November 8, 1979, she was driving to class on a rural highway when she was hit head-on by another car. It turned out that her best friend was driving the other car, and she died from a broken neck. Wilma's face was crushed, both of her legs were broken, as well as some of her ribs. For most of 1980 she was confined to a wheelchair and underwent seventeen operations on her face and legs. Just as she was beginning to recover and starting to walk again, she developed a paralyzing nerve disease called myasthenia gravis. Doctors removed her thyroid to treat the disease and gave her drug therapy.

Throughout this difficult time, friends and relatives rallied around Wilma. When she was finally ready to return to work in 1981, she did so with even stronger conviction about the importance of reaching out to help people in need.

Her first large project was in the community of Bell, a town devastated by unemployment (as high as 60 percent), drinking, and fighting. It was so isolated, residents did not have running water. Wilma managed to secure hundreds of thousands of dollars in federal funds to help the people of Bell rebuild their town. Community members did everything from raising additional funds to hauling lumber. She felt this sort of project was important because it put the community "in a position of assuming responsibility for change, and it builds pride. People develop a sense that they can indeed alter their lives and community."[8] A year later, Wilma established the Cherokee Nation Community Development Department and was named its first director.

In 1983 Ross Swimmer decided to run for his third four-year term as principal chief and asked Wilma to run as his deputy chief, a position comparable to vice president. Wilma accepted the offer and was surprised to discover that "there were some people who didn't think a woman should be in a position that high in the tribe."[9] She reminded voters that originally Cherokee women had a great deal of power. They "chose the chiefs and the chiefs served at the pleasure of the women."[10] It was after the Europeans arrived that the Cherokee "adopted a lot of ugly things that were part of the non-Indian world," she said, "and one of those things was sexism."[11]

In the end, Wilma Mankiller and Ross Swimmer managed to win the elections, and in August of 1983 Mankiller became the first female deputy chief of the Cherokee Nation. One of her duties was to preside over the monthly council meetings in which Cherokees could make suggestions, ask questions, and debate hot issues. The only woman at the table, Wilma quickly realized that some of the men were intent on not letting her speak. "Luckily I controlled the microphones," she laughed, "and each time I was interrupted, I just switched off their mikes. I think those members finally got the message that I was determined to be heard."[12]

Under her leadership, a number of Cherokee businesses were established, including a poultry ranch and an electronics company. She also raised money to expand the Cherokee Heritage Center museum, develop the Institute for Cherokee Literacy, and redesign the voting districts to make certain that people living in rural areas had equal representation in the government.

In 1985 President Ronald Reagan offered Ross Swimmer the job of director of the Bureau of Indian Affairs. When Swimmer left for Washington, the job of principal chief automatically passed to Wilma Mankiller since she was second-in-command. In December 1985, she was sworn in as the first woman chief. Because she had risen to this position without a mandate from the people she felt she "had all the responsibility with none of the authority. So mostly during that period I just coped."[13]

Her private life, on the other hand, was filled with joy because she had decided to marry again. Her husband was longtime friend Charley Soap, a full-blooded Cherokee, a skilled traditional dancer, and a Native American activist.

In 1987 Wilma Mankiller was coming to the end of her term as principal chief and felt ambivalent about running for reelection. She was frustrated by her squabbles with the council and tired of people criticizing her solely because she was a woman. As the election neared, more and more people came out to Mankiller Flats urging her not to run. Finally she said, "If one more family comes by and tells me not to run, I'm running."[14] When that family came, she threw her hat into the ring.

She knew it would be a tough race. Her three opponents were politically connected men. But she went from town to town tirelessly speaking with voters, listening to their concerns, and promising to do whatever she could to help them if elected. She managed to win the election with 56 percent of the vote. This time, as she was sworn into office, she knew that she had received a mandate from the people.

Wilma Mankiller worked hard to bring environmentally sound businesses into the community. She established a jobs corps center to help train Cherokees and to offer technical assistance and financial support to budding businesspeople. Under her leadership new health facilities were built and a Head Start program was established to help educate young Cherokee children.

When Mankiller ran for reelection in 1991, the Cherokees knew how much she had done for the Nation, and she won in a landslide with 83 percent of the vote. In her second full term, she focused on the needs of youths. She established a mentor program pairing teenage girls with women working in various fields. She also established youth shelters. "The youth, especially, are the future," she said. "We have to be careful we don't relax too much and watch our future disappear."[15]

In 1995 Wilma Mankiller decided not to seek reelection. "It was time for the Cherokee Nation to have a change," she said.[16] In 1996 she took a job teaching at Dartmouth College, in New Hampshire.

Her legacy, however, continues to live on, especially her belief that Cherokee people need to learn to believe they can succeed by helping themselves. "A big part of setting the stage for having people take control of their own lives and solve their own problems is getting people to believe they can," she has said. "Our folks are a long way away from uniformly believing that, after a couple hundred years of being told that other people have the best ideas for us."[17] Under Mankiller's leadership, Cherokees began taking steps toward realizing a brighter future where once again they have the freedom to be masters of their own destiny.

NINE

⬥

Vilma Martinez

In 1973 Vilma Martinez became the president and general counsel of the Mexican-American Legal Defense and Educational Fund (MALDEF), an organization that fights to secure civil and constitutional rights for millions of Mexican-Americans. When MALDEF was founded in 1968, Mexican-Americans were discriminated against in employment and often denied equal pay. In the Southwest, one third of all Mexican-American families were surviving on incomes below the poverty line. Many Mexican-American students were put in remedial classes because they did not understand English, and 50 percent of all young Mexican-Americans dropped out of school.[1]

"It is unfortunate," Vilma Martinez has said, "that, in our society, there is a tremendous amount of discrimination against Latinos. . . . One can cry and one can complain, which I did. But one can get angry, and do something about it. I decided to do something about it."[2]

⬥

Vilma Martinez was born on October 17, 1943. She grew up the oldest of five children. Her family spoke Spanish and lived in a poor neighborhood of San Antonio, Texas, where, Vilma said, "the big aspiration [goal] was to be a secretary."[3]

During childhood Vilma encountered the prejudices facing Hispanics. She said, "I remember as a child reading in the paper that a [Mexican-American] Congressman would not be served in a cafeteria. . . . I also remember that as a child we were going on a picnic to a state park, and, at the last minute, we were not allowed to go. I asked the priest why we were not going—we were all so excited about it. The priest said that they did not allow Mexican-Americans in the park."[4]

Vilma's parents never allowed her to think that such obstacles should keep her from succeeding in life. She said, "I grew up believing that if you had merit—and worked hard—it would be rewarded."[5] This belief was challenged when she encountered racial prejudice at school. Vilma recalled, "I walked into classrooms where the teachers looked at me and thought, 'Well she's Chicana, she can't be very bright. . . .' I had to deal with it and fight it all my life."[6]

In Vilma's neighborhood, Mexican-American children were channeled into the vocational high school rather than the college-preparatory school that white children attended. Vilma's junior high school counselor told her she "would be more comfortable [at the vocational school] and there would be more Mexican-Americans there."[7] Vilma shook her head and said, "But I don't want to be comfortable. I want to go to college. Please send my records to [the college preparatory school] immediately because I am going to show up there next fall!"[8] At this school, Vilma got straight A's.

In her junior year, when the other students were getting ready to apply for college, Vilma asked the academic adviser for help. No one in her family had ever gone to college, and she wasn't sure how to apply. The adviser ignored her. Finally,

Vilma decided to write to the University of Texas on her own and was accepted.

Vilma recalled that when she discussed with her father her plans to go to college, "my father told me that I would never make it, that I would get married and have children. I used to fight with him all the time, but I wasn't getting anywhere. Finally it occurred to me that if I was really going to deal with it, I would just have to go out there and prove it—just do it to prove to him I could achieve the goals that I had set for myself."[9]

When she arrived at the University of Texas, she threw herself into her studies, wanting to get her degree as quickly as possible. She was worried that something might happen to her father and, as the oldest child, she would be expected to come home and support the family. Taking evening classes, summer school courses, and correspondence classes, she earned a four-year degree in only two and a half years.

Upon graduating in 1964, she knew that she wanted to become a lawyer. She said, "I understood the part lawyers played in governing the country. I understood further we Latinos had little access to the law. . . . [Becoming a civil rights lawyer for Latinos] would be my contribution to the betterment of the Hispanic community."[10]

When she applied for a scholarship to Columbia Law School in New York City, the interviewer said, "Why should we give you a scholarship; you are a woman and you are going to be married and have children. We would have wasted our investment."[11] Vilma replied that she had been working too long and too hard to not practice law and won the scholarship. She was one of only twenty women in a class of three hundred.

Soon after graduating from Columbia in 1967, she married a fellow attorney named Stuart Singer. They had met in a class to prepare for the bar exam (the test all lawyers must pass before they are allowed to practice law). Vilma said that he was very supportive of her ambitions and added that "Stuart is the only man I ever met who said, 'Vilma, you're not tough enough.' That's just what I was waiting to hear."[12]

After passing the bar exam, Martinez took a job with the legal defense fund of the National Association for the Advancement of Colored People (NAACP). This organization protects the legal rights of African-Americans. She said, "I believe the discrimination against Hispanics and blacks is quite similar, and it must be seriously addressed."[13]

Working for the NAACP, she was struck by the vitality and influence of the black middle class, which helped to educate and bring hope to young African-Americans. She said, "I think [Mexican-Americans] have missed the kinds of support black communities have fostered for themselves. It is apparent that Mexican-Americans to a great extent are suffering from a lack of education, and it is equally apparent they lack a middle class to help them become a part of the mainstream society."[14] She wanted to do something to help the Hispanic community and to make sure that young Mexican-Americans were getting the education they deserved.

When a group of lawyers from Texas visited her office and told her that they were interested in establishing an organization that would protect the civil rights of Mexican-Americans, Vilma enthusiastically offered her support. MALDEF was born in 1968 with an initial grant of $2.2 million from the Ford Foundation.

The president of the Ford Foundation said, "In terms of legal enforcement of their civil rights, American citizens of Mexican descent are now where the Negro community was a quarter-century ago. . . . Because the law has often been used against Mexican-Americans as well as other minority groups, they are suspicious of legal proceedings."[15] He hoped that MALDEF would change this pattern.

Vilma helped with the group's establishment, but continued to work at the NAACP and later for the New York State Division of Human Rights. Between 1971 and 1973 she served as a trial lawyer for a Wall Street firm in New York City.

She has said that in each job she's had, "you have to establish your competence and credentials either because you are young, or you are a woman, or you are a Mexican-American—or all three."[16] She recalled that when she went to court with her law partner she was routinely mistaken for his secretary. Once the firm held a party at a private men's club to celebrate a victory. Martinez decided not to attend the affair after discovering that she would be expected to enter through a back door because she was a woman.

In 1973 the position of president and general counsel for MALDEF became available, and Martinez decided to apply for the job. She told the board of trustees that "what MALDEF needed was a hotshot litigator [lawyer] to build a high-powered legal firm."[17] Once she got the job, she moved with her husband to San Francisco, where MALDEF's headquarters were located.

Under Martinez's leadership, MALDEF rose to national prominence by addressing important constitutional issues, such as voting rights. In 1975 MALDEF pushed Congress to decree bilingual elections. Martinez argued that a significant number of Mexican-Americans who were U.S. citizens spoke little English. Since they could not read their ballots, the constitutional right to vote was being denied them. After hearing extensive testimony on the subject, Congress agreed, banning "English-only elections" wherever a significant number of Spanish-speaking people lived.

The provision was included as part of the Voting Rights Act, which had been originally established in 1965 to ban literacy tests and other tactics that had been used in the past to keep minorities from voting.

The Voting Rights Act was due to expire in 1981, and Martinez, on behalf of MALDEF, fought hard for its extension. Some members of Congress who opposed the bilingual provision proposed a clause to strip it from the act. They stated that the provision encouraged citizens not to learn English and that it cost too much money to have ballots printed in dual languages.

Martinez argued that costs of bilingual elections had decreased dramatically since 1976 and pointed out that even one longtime opponent had acknowledged that "beyond start-up costs, the sums are truly insignificant."[18] Further, Martinez stated that under the act, Hispanic registration had increased 64 percent in Texas, 38 percent in California, and 30 percent nationwide.[19] In the congressional vote, the clause stripping the bilingual provision was defeated 283 to 129, and the Voting Rights Act was extended until 1992.

Martinez further increased the power of the Hispanic vote by heading a task force in 1980 for President Jimmy Carter's administration that made certain that Mexican-Americans were properly counted in that year's census. In the 1970 census hundreds of thousands of Mexican-Americans had not been counted. By making certain that the 1980 census was more accurate, Martinez ensured that new voter districts were created in Hispanic communities. Because these districts were entitled to elect a representative, more Mexican-Americans joined the state legislatures.

Under Martinez's leadership, MALDEF addressed other important issues facing Hispanics such as the misuse of police force in dealing with Mexican-Americans and other minorities.

The Community Relations director for the Justice Department acknowledged that "problems stemming from police use of deadly force [against minorities] loom as one of the most serious and inflammatory community relations problems confronting the nation. . . . The issue has reached such

crisis proportions that in some parts of the country an unde-
clared war has seemingly developed between minorities and
the police."[20]

In 1979 a police report had found that in seven major
cities 78 percent of citizens who were shot and killed by police were minorities.[21] Another study found that the chances
of a minority person being shot by a policeman were eight
times greater than a white person being shot.[22] Martinez
charged that the Justice Department had not been prosecut-
ing the police officers who had been guilty of brutality and
that they had treated the problem with near indifference.

As a result of protests by MALDEF and other organizations, the Justice Department agreed to form a multiracial
coalition to address the problem, and all across the country
seminars on deadly force were held for police officials.

Under Martinez's leadership, MALDEF also responded to
1977 reports that armed members of the Ku Klux Klan were
patrolling sections of the border between Mexico and the
United States. David Duke, the president of the Knights of the
Ku Klux Klan, stated there would be between 500 and 1,000
Klansmen searching for Mexican immigrants attempting to
cross illegally onto U.S. soil. With MALDEF's urging, Attorney
General Griffen Bell ordered members of the Klan to disband
their patrols and to leave the policing of the borders to law
enforcement officials. The Klan gradually withdrew.

One of Martinez's greatest concerns has always been education. She said, "It is extraordinarily sad . . . that Mexican-
American children are told they won't succeed, and they
shouldn't get their hopes up."[23] She realized that for many
children language was a major barrier. Those who were not
fluent in English had more trouble learning and keeping up
with their peers. Sometimes these students would be inaccu-
rately assumed to be learning-disabled.

Martinez and MALDEF argued and won a lawsuit that
charged that children in public schools should have the right

to receive a bilingual education. It is believed this helps level the playing field so that while these students are learning English, they are also continuing to progress in their studies in their native languages. Martinez felt this was one of the great achievements of her career, but said that when "I went to Texas to investigate the situation, I found that . . . the children were not receiving [a bilingual education] because the community did not have the support organization to make sure that consistent pressure was being put on the school system [to follow the law]. This made me realize that MALDEF should be much more than a legal service, and become a community representative."[24]

Martinez helped to expand the role of MALDEF to provide Mexican-Americans with resources and community education programs in addition to legal services. The organization grew to employ a staff of eighty with six offices across the country and an annual budget of $2.5 million.

In 1982 Martinez decided to step down as the head of MALDEF. She returned to private practice at a law firm in Los Angeles, where she continues to work. She and Stuart Singer are also the parents of two sons.

In 1984 she became the second woman and first Chicana to serve on the Board of Regents of the University of California. This board addresses issues affecting the University of California system and makes recommendations. "You have to read the reports given to you very carefully," she said, "[and] evaluate what is there and come to your own decision about a wide variety of issues. . . . Then you have to speak out to the full board—and, win or lose, you must make yourself heard."[25]

Many have noted that when Vilma Martinez speaks, she does so forcefully but without ever raising her voice. Her husband has remarked, "Lots of people can be loud. The key is to be effective."[26] Her effectiveness has been recognized by many.

Throughout her career Vilma Martinez has won many honors and awards. During President Carter's administration she was asked to serve on a committee to help pick U.S. ambassadors. Governor Edmund Brown of California asked her to help pick judges for the state's courts. In 1976 she was given the American Institute Thomas Jefferson Award in recognition of her contributions to public service. Two years later, she was awarded Columbia University's Medal for Excellence.

Vilma Martinez has said, "I am successful because I have the confidence, courage and willingness to work hard for what I want."[27]

TEN

※

ELEANOR HOLMES NORTON

When Eleanor Holmes Norton was working as an attorney for the American Civil Liberties Union (ACLU), she encountered one of the great ironies of American democracy—that the freedom of speech granted to all citizens under the First Amendment of the Constitution also gives people the right to speak in opposition to the American ideal that all men and women are created equal. As a woman who had struggled against racism and sexism in her own life, Norton found herself in the uncomfortable position of defending the freedom of speech of white supremacists. She said, "There are certain substantive principles that I believe in strongly. One is racial equality. The other is free speech. As it turns out, if I want to implement the principle of equality, I do it through participation in the civil rights movement. To implement my belief in free speech, I represent anyone whose free speech has been infringed."[1]

※

Eleanor Holmes was born on June 13, 1937, in Washington, D.C. Both of her parents were college graduates—her father worked as a civil servant for the housing department and her mother was a teacher. They impressed upon Eleanor the importance of getting a good education and expected her to go on to college. Eleanor recalled that as the eldest of three girls, "I was treated as if more was expected of me and therefore I internalized a sense of striving and responsibility."[2]

She grew up in a close-knit African-American neighborhood, where the entire community took on the responsibility of helping to raise the children. Eleanor knew she could always turn to neighbors when she needed help. She knew when she was outside playing with her friends, there were adults who were keeping an eye out for them and making certain that they were behaving. These adults also helped the children have a positive sense of self-worth, despite the racial prejudices and discrimination they often encountered.

At the time, schools were still segregated, and Eleanor attended the only college preparatory high school for blacks in the city. She recalled, "I was raised to think that when you couldn't go to the white schools . . . [you were] superior to those who kept you from those schools."[3]

She graduated as one of the top students in Dunbar High School in 1955 and enrolled as a science major at Antioch College in Yellow Springs, Ohio. In 1960 she earned a bachelor's degree in history and knew that she wanted to become a civil rights lawyer. Inspired by the oratory of Martin Luther King, Jr., and the budding civil rights movement, Eleanor went on to Yale University and acquired a master's in American history and a law degree at the same time.

In 1964 after graduating from Yale, she moved to Philadelphia, where she clerked for a federal judge for a year. During this time, she met a handsome naval officer named Edward Norton. He fully accepted her plans to pursue a career in the law, and on October 9, 1965, they were married.

That same year, the newlyweds moved to New York City, where Eleanor took a job as assistant legal director of the American Civil Liberties Union. The ACLU's policy is to support everyone's right to free speech and press, regardless of the person's point of view.

During her five years working at the ACLU, Eleanor Norton represented a wide range of clients, including feminists, Vietnam War protesters, and George Wallace, the governor of Alabama. Wallace opposed the civil rights movement and school integration. During President John F. Kennedy's administration, he had tried to prevent blacks from entering the University of Alabama. In 1968 Wallace ran for president as the American Independent Party's candidate. He won sizable support, but when he tried to hold a rally at Shea Stadium in New York City, it was feared that a race riot might ensue and he was denied a permit for the rally. Norton successfully argued in court that this denied Wallace his right to free speech.

In October 1968 she argued and won her first case before the Supreme Court. Norton was representing the National States' Rights Party, a group of white supremacists who, two years earlier, had wanted to hold a rally in Maryland. Local government and law enforcement officials had refused to grant them a permit, fearing that their hateful condemnations of blacks, women, and Jews could incite violence between the white supremacists and protesters.

Handling this case was difficult for Eleanor. She despised the things the white supremacists said, and yet she felt that it was her duty to make certain that the First Amendment applied equally to everyone in society. She explained, "There's no way to argue, nor should there be, that black people ought to have freedom of speech but racists shouldn't. If the principle is going to live at all, it's got to live for anybody who wants to exercise it."[4]

While working at the ACLU, Eleanor Norton also initiated

one of the early sex-discrimination cases against a major national weekly news magazine and won promotions for sixty women employees.

In 1970 the mayor of New York City appointed Eleanor as head of the city's Commission on Human Rights. This organization represented citizens who had experienced various forms of discrimination. At a press conference, Eleanor stated that one of her priorities would be "to see that nondiscrimination becomes a reality for women."[5]

She fought successfully for more-liberal maternity benefits on behalf of a woman who worked in a blue-collar job, a woman who worked for an airline, and a woman who worked in a bank. She also fought for the right of a female sports reporter to sit with the male reporters in the press box at a hockey stadium. In a well-publicized case, she forced an expensive restaurant to serve women on an equal basis with men. She also forced a hotel to allow women access to the "Men's Bar" and to change the name of that bar. During her tenure at the Commission on Human Rights, she also gave birth to two children—her daughter, Katherine, and her son, John.

In 1977 President Jimmy Carter appointed Norton as the head of the Equal Employment Opportunity Commission (EEOC). This commission is charged with enforcing Title VII of the 1964 Civil Rights Act, prohibiting job discrimination based on race, color, religion, sex, or national origin. The EEOC also has the authority to issue guidelines for the entire nation telling employers how certain legal statutes related to employment will be interpreted.

When Norton arrived, the organization had a reputation for inefficiency. She discovered that there was a backlog of 130,000 unresolved cases and that it was taking, on average, a year and a half for a single case to be investigated. Norton immediately set to work reorganizing the EEOC. She increased productivity at the organization by 65 percent, and under her leadership the average case was being completed in less than two months.

Norton used her position as the head of the EEOC to address the issue of sexual harassment in the workplace. At the time, there was a "boys will be boys" attitude at many job sites. Employers felt that sexual harassment was a women's problem and that it was not something they should be responsible for addressing. It had taken a decade after the passage of Title VII before the first sexual harassment suits reached the courts, and the earliest ones that did had not convinced the courts that sexual harassment was a form of discrimination.

In a 1976 case, however, a court found that sexual harassment could be equated with discrimination if a woman could manage to prove that she had lost her job, or was refused a promotion, or in some other concrete way had been discriminated against because of her sex. For instance, a woman would have to demonstrate that she had lost her job because she had rebuffed her boss's sexual advances.

Norton felt that this interpretation of the law was too narrow. In 1980, under her leadership, the EEOC released the groundbreaking "Guidelines on Discrimination Because of Sex." These broader guidelines stated that sexual discrimination included all acts of harassment through sexual speech or behavior that created an intimidating or antagonistic environment for the targeted employee. It made clear that employers were responsible for addressing sexual harassment within their workplaces.

Norton stated that such a "guideline is like a law. . . . If someone says this party isn't abiding by it, a complaint is filed. If an employer refuses to meet the terms of the conciliation, then the EEOC has the authority to go into court [and fight on behalf of the person making the complaint]."[6]

In 1981 a court affirmed the EEOC's "Guidelines on Sexual Harassment." The importance of these new guidelines was made clear when that same year *Redbook* magazine published a survey which found that 85 percent of respondents had experienced sexual harassment at work.[7]

Norton's tenure at the EEOC came to an end in 1981 when Ronald Reagan became president and appointed a fellow Republican, Clarence Thomas, as head of the department.

Norton taught law at Georgetown University Law Center in Washington, D.C., until 1990, when she decided to run for elected office as the district's delegate in the House of Representatives. The former delegate, Walter Fauntroy, had given up this seat after nearly twenty years to run unsuccessfully for mayor of the city.

Norton began her campaign with a sizable lead, but shortly before the election, it was revealed that she had not filed local income taxes for a period of seven years. At a press conference, she tearfully acknowledged that her husband had been in charge of the family finances and was responsible for the mistake. While she lost some votes, she still won the election by a wide margin. Two weeks after the election, Eleanor separated from her husband, and they were eventually divorced.

The position of D.C. delegate is an unusual one because Washington, D.C., is an unusual city. Unlike all other cities, it does not belong to a state and is governed by Congress. The D.C. delegate (like the delegates from the U.S.-held areas of Guam, Puerto Rico, the Virgin Islands, and American Samoa) is known as a "nonvoting" representative because this person is not allowed to vote on pieces of legislation brought before the entire House of Representatives.

When Norton took office, Washington, D.C., was facing some serious problems. Since 1986, crack cocaine had been a major problem for the city, and as a result, crime was on the rise. Between 1985 and 1991 the homicide rate rose 260 percent. The city had gotten the nickname "the Murder Capital."[8]

During the past thirty years, the population of Washington had dropped by a third.[9] Most of the people leaving were fleeing crime and poor schools, but they were those who could afford to do so—the middle and upper classes.

Norton, as well as a number of other people from the district, felt that one solution would be for the district to become a state. She argued that because of D.C.'s unique position as a stateless city, an unfair tax burden was placed on the residents. She pointed to the fact that in other troubled cities across the country, states help to pay for some city services. Money that these states collect from taxes paid by the wealthy neighborhoods is cycled to these poorer areas to help pay for such things as schools and police forces. But in Washington there is no state to help defer the costs of the city's services. Norton has said, "It is remarkable that District taxpayers have been able to carry this . . . burden as long as they have."[10]

One of the main reasons that D.C. has not become a state is that the district is heavily Democratic. If it became a state, it would be entitled to elect voting members to the House and Senate. The 1994 Republican-controlled Congress made it clear that it had no intention of granting the Democratic district statehood.

To ease the city's tax burdens, Norton came up with a controversial proposal that would give the city a significant federal tax break in 1995. She suggested that residents should continue to pay local taxes but that most should get a tax break on their federal taxes by paying a flat 15 percent. Norton reasoned that this would encourage middle-class people who had fled the city to return because they would pay lower federal taxes in D.C. than they would elsewhere. If higher-income people moved back to the city, they in turn would provide a higher tax base for local taxes and relieve some of D.C.'s financial problems.

Norton's proposal won support from many Republican leaders, including the House and Senate majority leaders, who saw it as a way to stimulate economic growth in the city. However, it was opposed by Democratic President Bill Clinton's administration, which pointed out that it would cost the federal government about $750 million a year in lost revenues. The Republican chairman of the House Ways and Means Committee (which writes tax laws) also warned there would be "a furor around the country" when citizens from other cities (who pay up to 39.6 percent of their income in federal taxes) found out that D.C.'s residents were going to pay only a flat 15 percent.[11] Today, Norton's proposal is still under consideration by Congress, and she continues to serve as the delegate from D.C.

She has said, "You could say race was an obstacle to me, you could say sex was an obstacle to me, but I refused to own them in that way. I was black and female, but I never conceived that those [facts] were supposed to keep me from doing what I wanted to do."[12]

SOURCE NOTES

ONE: MARGARETHE CAMMERMEYER

1. Margarethe Cammermeyer, *Serving in Silence* (New York: Viking, 1994), 305.

2. Ibid., 13.

3. Ibid., 21.

4. Ibid., 49.

5. Ibid., 97.

6. Ibid., 165.

7. Ron Arias and Joan DeClaire, "Fighting Back," *People Weekly*, June 15, 1992, 54.

8. Michael H. Hodges, "They Asked, She Told," *Detroit News*, April 4, 1995, C1, from 1995 CD Newsbank Comprehensive.

9. Patti Doten, "The Decorated Officer Fights to Reconcile her Gay Identity and the Career She Loves," *Boston Globe*, January 3, 1995, 29, from 1995 CD Newsbank Comprehensive.

10. Ibid.

11. Cammermeyer, *Serving in Silence*, 230.

12. Arias, "Fighting Back," 54.

13. Ibid., 51.

14. Cammermeyer, *Serving in Silence*, 274.

15. Ibid., 276.

16. Ibid., 292.

17. Ibid., 300.

18. Ibid., 305.

19. Hodges, "They Asked, She Told," C1.

20. Doten, "The Decorated Officer Fights to Reconcile her Gay Identity and the Career She Loves," 29.

TWO: MARIAN WRIGHT EDELMAN

1. David G. Savage, "Tens of Thousands Rally in Defense of Aid to Children," *Los Angeles Times*, June 2, 1996, A12.

2. Richette L. Haywood, "Marian Wright Edelman: First Mom," *Ebony*, May 1996, 150–152.

3. Joann J. Burch, *Marian Wright Edelman: Children's Champion* (Brookfield, Conn.: The Millbrook Press, 1994), 7.

4. Marian Wright Edelman, *The Measure of Our Success: A Letter to My Children and Yours* (Boston: Beacon Press, 1992), 5.

5. Beatrice Siegel, *Marian Wright Edelman: The Making of a Crusader* (New York: Simon and Schuster, 1995), 26.

6. Steve Otfinoski, *Marian Wright Edelman: Defender of Children's Rights* (Woodbridge, Conn.: Blackbirch Press, 1991), 21.

7. Judith Viorst, "The Woman Behind the First Lady," *Redbook*, June 1993, 66.

8. Otfinoski, *Marian Wright Edelman*, 28.

9. Siegel, *Marian Wright Edelman*, 80.

10. Ibid., 93.

11. Otfinoski, *Marian Wright Edelman*, 36.

12. Siegel, *Marian Wright Edelman*, 103.

13. Otfinoski, *Marian Wright Edelman*, 4.

14. Calvin Tomkins, "Profiles: A Sense of Urgency," *New Yorker*, March 1989, 70.

15. Siegel, *Marian Wright Edelman*, 117.

16. Viorst, "The Woman Behind the First Lady," 64–66.

17. "Children of a Lesser Country," *New Yorker*, January 15, 1996, 25.

18. Neil A. Lewis, "A Friendship in Tatters Over Policy," *New York Times*, September 13, 1996, A26.

19. Elizabeth Gleick, "The Children's Crusade," *Time*, June 3, 1996, 33.

20. Haywood, "Marian Wright Edelman," 156.

THREE: MYRLIE EVERS-WILLIAMS

1. Brian Lanker, I *Dream a World* (New York: Stewart, Tabori, and Chang, 1989), 94.

2. Mrs. Medgar Evers with William Peters, *For Us, The Living* (Garden City, N.Y.: Doubleday, 1967), 35.

3. Ibid., 41–42.

4. Ibid., 46.

5. Marilyn Marshall, "Myrlie Evers Remembers: 25 Years After Assassination of Civil Rights Legend," *Ebony*, June, 1988, 114.

6. Claudia Dreifus, "The Widow Gets Her Verdict," *New York Times Magazine*, November 27, 1994, 70.

7. Maryanne Vollers, *Ghosts of Mississippi: The Murder of Medgar Evers, The Trials of Byron De La Beckwith, and The Haunting of the New South* (Boston: Little, Brown, 1995), 107.

8. Dreifus, "The Widow Gets Her Verdict," 70.

9. Ibid.

10. Ibid.

11. Steven V. Roberts, "Mrs. Medgar Evers: A New Life But Bitter Memories Linger," *New York Times*, March 26, 1970, 60.

12. Jill Petty, "Myrlie Evers-Williams," *Ms*, January/February 1996, 43.

13. Jack E. White, "A Matter of Life and Death," *Time*, February 27, 1995, 23.

14. Dreifus, "The Widow Gets Her Verdict," 70.

15. Catherine Manegold, "She Has a Dream," *Harper's Bazaar*, July 1995, 58.

16. White, "A Matter of Life and Death," 23.

17. Lydia Lum, "NAACP Chief Urges Women, Minorities to Go to Polls," *Houston Chronicle*, October 27, 1995, 33, from 1996 CD Newsbank Comprehensive.

18. Manegold, "She Has a Dream," 59.

19. Michael A. Fletcher, "Mfume Takes NAACP Helm Today," *Washington Post*, February 15, 1996, A3, from 1996 CD Newsbank Comprehensive.

20. James Bock, "Mfume Takes Office as Head of an NAACP Living Within its Means," *The Sun*, February 18, 1996, 3A, from 1996 CD Newsbank Comprehensive.

21. Petty, "Myrlie Evers-Williams," 43.

FOUR: ELIZABETH GLASER

1. Patricia McCormick, "Living with AIDS," *Parents Magazine*, November 1993, 46.

2. Elizabeth Glaser and Laura Palmer, *In the Absence of Angels: A Hollywood Family's Courageous Story* (New York: Putnam, 1991), 18.

3. Ibid., 26.

4. Ibid., 46.

5. McCormick, "Living with AIDS," 42.

6. Glaser and Palmer, *In the Absence of Angels*, 60.

7. McCormick, "Living with AIDS," 42.

8. Glaser and Palmer, *In the Absence of Angels*, 54.

9. Ibid., 115.

10. Ibid., 127.

11. Ibid., 137.

12. McCormick, "Living with AIDS," 44.

13. Ibid., 46.

14. Kristin McMurran, "After the Tragedy, A Call to Arms," *People Weekly*, February 4, 1991, 96.

15. Kathie Berlin, "My Friend Elizabeth," *Ladies' Home Journal*, March 1996, 196.

16. "Elizabeth Glaser Dies at 47," Associated Press, December 3, 1994, from 1995 CD Newsbank Comprehensive.

17. David Ellis, "The Defiant One," *People Weekly*, December 19, 1994, 53.

FIVE: DELORES HUERTA

1. Kathleen Bowman, *New Women in Politics* (Chicago: Childrens Press, 1976), 16.

2. Barbara L. Baer and Glenna Matthews, "The Women of the Boycott," *The Nation*, February 23, 1974, 236.

3. Dan Webster, "Farm Fighter," *Spokesman Review*, November 14, 1995, from 1995 CD Newsbank Comprehensive.

4. Dick Meister and Anne Loftis, *A Long Time Coming: The Struggle to Unionize America's Farm Workers* (New York: Macmillan, 1977), 118.

5. Jacques Levy, *Cesar Chavez: Autobiography of La Causa* (New York: Norton, 1975), 95.

6. Dana Catherine de Ruiz and Richard Larios, *La Causa: The Migrant Farmworkers' Story* (New York: Steck-Vaughn, 1993), 26.

7. Webster, "Farm Fighter."

8. Baer and Matthews, "The Women of the Boycott," 233–234.

9. Ibid., 237.

10. Meister and Loftis, A *Long Time Coming*, 151.

11. Baer and Matthews, "The Women of the Boycott," 238.

12 Webster, "Farm Fighter."

13. Meister and Loftis, A *Long Time Coming*, 164.

14. Ibid., 168.

15. Ibid., 219.

16. Kimber Williams, "Activist Gets Record Sum for Beating," *Register Guard*, March 19, 1991, from 1991 CD Newsbank Comprehensive.

17. Baer and Loftis, "The Women of the Boycott," 238.

SIX: PATRICIA IRELAND

1. Victoria Benning, "NOW Votes to Keep Ireland as President," *Boston Globe*, July 5, 1993, 16, from 1993 CD Newsbank Comprehensive.

2. Patricia Ireland, *What Women Want* (New York: Dutton, 1996), 15.

3. Jane Gross, "Patricia Ireland, President of NOW: Does She Speak for Today's Women?," *New York Times Magazine*, March 1, 1992, 38.

4. Ireland, *What Women Want*, 25.

5. Ibid., 31.

6. Lisa Collier Cool, "The New Leadership," *Cosmopolitan*, May 1994, 206.

7. Ireland, *What Women Want*, 45.

8. Eleanor J. Bader, "A Leader for NOW," *Progressive*, July 1996, 44.

9. Cool, "The New Leadership," 206.

10. Gross, "Patricia Ireland, President of NOW," 38.

11. Ireland, *What Women Want*, 87.

12. Ibid., 104.

13. Ibid., 122.

14. Ibid., 132.

15. Gross, "Patricia Ireland, President of NOW," 38.

16. Judith Graham, ed., *Current Biography Yearbook*, 1992 (New York: H. W. Wilson, 1992), 287.

17. Gross, "Patricia Ireland, President of NOW," 18.

18. Howard Fineman, "Shaking Things Up at NOW," *Newsweek* July 22, 1991, 24.

19 Benning, "NOW Votes to Keep Ireland as President," 16.

20."Government Seeks RICO-Abortion Rule," Associated Press, May 21, 1993, from 1993 CD Newsbank Comprehensive.

21. Joyce Price, "NOW Rally Protests 'Contract,' Violence Against Women," *Washington Times*, April 9, 1995, A3, from 1995 CD Newsbank Comprehensive.

22. Ellen O'Brien, "NOW Goes Against the Grain With a New and Expanded ERA," *Philadelphia Inquirer*, August 2, 1995, from 1996 CD Newsbank Comprehensive.

23. Gross, "Patricia Ireland, President of NOW," 16.

24. Ibid., 18.

SEVEN: MAGGIE KUHN

1. Francesca Lyman, "Maggie Kuhn: A Wrinkled Radical's Crusade," *Progressive*, January 1988, 29.

2. Ibid.

3. Maggie Kuhn with Christina Long and Laura Quinn, *No Stone Unturned: The Life and Times of Maggie Kuhn* (New York: Ballantine Books, 1991), 21.

4. Ibid., 34.

5. Ibid., 64.

6. Ibid., 104.

7. Charles Moritz, ed., *Current Biography Yearbook*, 1978 (New York: H. W. Wilson, 1978), 240.

8. Kuhn with Long and Quinn, *No Stone Unturned*, 131.

9. "How to Fight Age Bias," *Ms.*, June 1975, 91.

10. Jane Daugherty, "Whatever Happened to the Gray Panthers?" *50 Plus*, October 1983, 25.

11. Kuhn with Long and Quinn, *No Stone Unturned*, 149.

12. Ibid., 144.

13. "How to Fight Age Bias," 91.

14. Helen Benedict, "My Side: Maggie Kuhn," *Working Woman*, May 1982, 30.

15. Kuhn with Long and Quinn, *No Stone Unturned*, 196.

16. Ibid., 232.

EIGHT: WILMA MANKILLER

1. Wilma Mankiller and Michael Wallis, *Mankiller: A Chief and Her People* (New York: St. Martin's Press, 1993), 112.

2. Michele Wallace, "Wilma Mankiller," *Ms.*, January 1988, 69.

3. David Van Biema with Michael Wallis, "Activist Wilma Mankiller Is Set to Become the First Female Chief of the Cherokee Nation," *People Weekly*, December 2, 1985, 91.

4. Melissa Schwarz, *Wilma Mankiller: Principal Chief of the Cherokees* (New York: Chelsea House, 1994), 45.

5. Ibid., 49.

6. Van Biema with Wallis, "The First Female Chief of the Cherokee Nation," 92.

7. Schwarz, *Wilma Mankiller*, 13.

8. "People Expect Me to Be More Warlike," U.S. *News and World Report*, February 17, 1986, 64.

9. M. K. Gregory, "Wilma Mankiller: Harnessing Traditional Cherokee Wisdom," *Ms.*, August 1986, 32.

10. Ibid.

11. Wallace, "Wilma Mankiller," 68.

12. Della A. Yannuzzi, *Wilma Mankiller: Leader of the Cherokee Nation* (Hillside, N.J.: Enslow, 1994), 52.

13. Wallace, "Wilma Mankiller," 68.

14. Schwarz, *Wilma Mankiller*, 88.

15. Yannuzzi, *Wilma Mankiller*, 78.

16. "Cherokee Chief Stepping Down," Associated Press, June 16, 1995, from 1995 CD Newsbank Comprehensive.

17. Schwarz, *Wilma Mankiller*, 105.

NINE: VILMA MARTINEZ

1. Kathleen Teltsch, "Grant Aids Latins in the Southwest," *New York Times*, May 2, 1968, 38.

2. Al Carlos Hernández, "Vilma Martinez: Una Chicana Ejemplar," *Nuestro*, August/September 1981, 14.

3. Carol Lawson, "A Quiet but Effective Fighter for Mexican-American Rights," *New York Times*, May 19, 1978, A14.

4. Hernández, "Vilma Martinez," 13.

5. Dean Johnson, "Chair of the Board," *Nuestro*, September 1985, 36.

6. Hernández, "Vilma Martinez," 14.

7. Ibid.

8. Corinn Codye, *Vilma Martinez* (Milwaukee: Raintree, 1990), 9.

9. Hernández, "Vilma Martinez," 14.

10. Ibid.

11. Ibid.

12. Lawson, "A Quiet but Effective Fighter," A14.

13. Johnson, "Chair of the Board," 36.

14. Ibid.

15. Teltsch, "Grant Aids Latins in the Southwest," 38.

16. Lawson, "A Quiet but Effective Fighter," A14.

17. Hernández, "Vilma Martinez," 13.

18. Vilma S. Martinez, "A Democracy in Any Language," *New York Times*, October 1, 1981, 34.

19. Ibid.

20. Thomas A. Johnson, "U.S. Agency Moves to Head Off Racial Conflicts Over Allegations of Police Misuse of Force," *New York Times*, August 11, 1979, 6.

21. Ibid., 6.

22. Thomas A. Johnson, "Seminar for Police to Discuss Killings," *New York Times*, July 26, 1979, 12.

23. Johnson, "Chair of the Board," 36.

24. Hernández, "Vilma Martinez," 13.

25. Johnson, "Chair of the Board," 36.

26. Lawson, "A Quiet but Effective Fighter," A14.

27. Hernández, "Vilma Martinez," 13.

TEN: ELEANOR HOLMES NORTON

1. Charles Moritz, ed., *Current Biography Yearbook*, 1976 (New York: H. W. Wilson, 1976), 295.

2. Brian Lanker, *I Dream a World: Portraits of Black Women Who Changed America* (New York: Stewart, Tabori, and Chang, 1989), 147.

3. Ibid.

4. Kathryn Cullen-Dupont, *The Encyclopedia of Women's History in America* (New York: Facts on File, 1996), 155.

5. Ibid.

6. Ann Curran, "Eleanor Holmes Norton: Job Bias," *Working Woman*, March 1980, 46.

7. Constance Jones, *Library in a Book: Sexual Harassment* (New York: Facts on File, 1996), 11.

8. Blaine Harden, "A City in Transition," *Washington Post*, June 18, 1995, A19, from 1995 CD Newsbank Comprehensive.

9. "Growth Serum for D.C.," *Wall Street Journal*, July 25, 1996, A20.

10. Michael A. Fletcher, "New Angle on Statehood," *Washington Post*, February 2, 1995, J1, from 1995 CD Newsbank Comprehensive.

11. "Growth Serum for D.C.," A20.

12. Lanker, I *Dream a World*, 147.

FURTHER READING

Bowman, Kathleen. *New Women in Politics*. Chicago: Childrens Press, 1976.

Burch, Joann J. *Marian Wright Edelman: Children's Champion*. Brookfield, Conn.: The Millbrook Press, 1994.

Cammermeyer, Margarethe. *Serving in Silence*. New York: Viking, 1994.

Codye, Corinn. *Vilma Martinez*. Milwaukee: Raintree, 1990.

De Ruiz, Dana Catherine, and Richard Larios. *La Causa: The Migrant Farmworkers' Story*. New York: Steck-Vaughn, 1993.

Edelman, Marian Wright. *The Measure of Our Success: A Letter to My Children and Yours*. Boston: Beacon Press, 1992.

Evers, Mrs. Medgar, with William Peters. *For Us, The Living*. Garden City, N.Y.: Doubleday, 1967.

Foner, Philip S. *Women and the American Labor Movement: From World War I to the Present*. New York: The Free Press, 1980.

Glaser, Elizabeth, and Laura Palmer. *In the Absence of Angels: A Hollywood Family's Courageous Story*. New York: Putnam, 1991.

Glassman, Bruce. *Wilma Mankiller: Chief of the Cherokee Nation*. New York: Blackbirch Press, 1992.

Ireland, Patricia. *What Women Want*. New York: Dutton, 1996.

Kuhn, Maggie, with Christina Long and Laura Quinn. *No Stone Unturned: *The Life and Times of Maggie Kuhn*. New York: Ballantine Books, 1991.

Lanker, Brian. *I Dream a World: Portraits of Black Women Who Changed America*. New York: Stewart, Tabori, and Chang, 1989.

Levy, Jacques. *Cesar Chavez: Autobiography of La Causa*. New York: Norton, 1975.

London, Joan, and Henry Anderson. *So Shall Ye Reap: The Story of Cesar Chavez and the Farm Workers' Movement*. New York: Thomas Y. Crowell Co., 1970.

Mankiller, Wilma, and Michael Wallis. *Mankiller: A Chief and Her People*. New York: St. Martin's Press, 1993.

Matthiessen, Peter. *Sal Si Puedes: Cesar Chavez and the New American Revolution*. New York: Dell, 1969.

Meister, Dick, and Anne Loftis. *A Long Time Coming: The Struggle to Unionize America's Farm Workers*. New York: Macmillan, 1977.

Otfinoski, Steve. *Marian Wright Edelman: Defender of Children's Rights*. Woodbridge, Conn.: Blackbirch Press, 1991.

Schwarz, Melissa. *Wilma Mankiller: Principal Chief of the Cherokees*. New York: Chelsea House, 1994.

Siegel, Beatrice. *Marian Wright Edelman: The Making of a Crusader*. New York: Simon and Schuster, 1995.

Vollers, Maryanne. *Ghosts of Mississippi: The Murder of Medgar Evers, The Trials of Byron De La Beckwith, and The Haunting of the New South*. Boston: Little, Brown, 1995.

Yannuzzi, Della A. *Wilma Mankiller: Leader of the Cherokee Nation*. Hillside, N.J.: Enslow, 1994.

INDEX

Agricultural Labor Relations Board, 58–59

AIDS, 41, 44–49

Alcatraz, 87

American Civil Liberties Union (ACLU), 103, 105

American Independent Party, 105

American Medical Association (AMA), 80–81

American Workers Organizing Committee (AWOC), 54, 56

Armed Services Committee, 16

Army, U.S., 7, 9–16

Atlantic Richfield Company, 36

Barnett, Ross, 35

Bradley, Tom, 36

Brown, Edmund, 58–59, 101

Bureau of Indian Affairs (BIA), 85, 90

Bush, George, 59, 67, 68

Cammermeyer, Margarethe, 7–17

Carter, Jimmy, 98, 101, 106

Chavez, Cesar, 53–55, 58

Cherokee Nation, 83–85, 87–91

Child Development Group of Mississippi (CDGM), 23

Children's Defense Fund (CDF), 25–27

Clinton, Bill, 15–16, 25, 27, 28, 49, 110

Clinton, Hillary Rodham, 25, 27

Close, Glenn, 16

Congress, U.S., 15–16, 25, 27–28, 38, 47, 65, 66, 68, 70, 98, 108–10

Constitution, U.S., First Amendment to, 103, 105

Consultation of Older and Younger Adults for Social Change, 78

De La Beckwith, Byron, 35, 37

Defense Department, U.S., 7, 14

Democratic Party, 36, 39, 49, 68, 69, 109, 110

Edelman, Marian Wright, 19–29
Edelman, Peter, 24, 25, 28
Eisner, Michael, 48
Equal Employment Opportunity Commission (EEOC), 106–8
Equal Rights Amendment (ERA), 65–66, 70
Evers, Medgar, 31, 33–35
Evers-Williams, Myrlie, 31–39

Farm Workers Association (FWA), 53–54
Fauntroy, Walter, 108
Ferraro, Geraldine, 68
Freedom Summer, 22

General Accounting Office, 15
Gingrich, Newt, 70
Glaser, Ariel, 41, 43–49
Glaser, Elizabeth, 41–49
Glaser, Jake, 43, 44, 47, 49
Glaser, Paul Michael, 41–45, 47, 48
Gray Panthers, 73, 78–81
Guimarra Corporation, 56

Head Start, 23, 25, 28, 42, 91
Hill, Anita, 68
Hitler, Adolf, 8
House of Representatives, 108, 109
Huerta, Delores, 51–59

Ireland, Patricia, 61–70

Jackson, Andrew, 84
Jackson, Hobart, 78

John Birch Society, 36
Johnson, Lyndon, 23
Justice Department, U.S., 98–99

Kennedy, John F., 35, 105
Kennedy, Robert F., 23, 24
King, Martin Luther, Jr., 24, 55, 104
Kuhn, Maggie, 73–81
Ku Klux Klan, 22

Lipscomb, Glenard P., 36
Los Angeles Board of Public Works, 36
Los Angeles Children's Museum, 43

Mankiller, Wilma, 83–91
Martinez, Vilma, 93–101
Media Watch, 80
Mexican-American Legal Defense and Educational Fund (MALDEF), 93, 96–100
Mfume, Kweisi, 39
Mississippi Sovereignty Commission, 37
Mondale, Walter, 68

Nader, Ralph, 79
National Association for the Advancement of Colored People (NAACP), 31, 33–35, 37–39, 59, 96, 97
National Association of Broadcasters, 80
National Coalition for Nursing Home Reform, 80
National Farm Workers Association (NFWA), 54–56

National Institute of Health, 47

National Organization for Women (NOW), 61, 64–70

National Shared Housing Resource Center, 81

National States' Rights Party, 105

National Women's Education Fund, 36

Nazis, 8

New York City Commission on Human Rights, 106

New York State Division of Human Rights, 97

Nixon, Richard, 25, 78, 87

Norton, Eleanor Holmes, 103–10

Nunn, Sam, 16

Nwangaza, Efia, 69

Ohlones Tribe, 87

Operation Rescue, 67

Pediatric Aids Foundation (PAF), 42, 48–49

Persian Gulf War, 12

Pit River Tribe, 87

Pregnancy Prevention Clearing House, 26

Project Stand Up for Women, 67

Reagan, Nancy, 48

Reagan, Ronald, 26, 48, 67, 90, 108

Republican Party, 36, 38, 67, 69, 108–10

Resurrection City, 24

Retired Professional Action Group, 79

Ross, Fred, 52, 53

Select Committee on Aging, 80

Senate, U.S., 109

Smeal, Eleanor, 66–67

Spielberg, Steven, 48

Stockton Community Service Organization (CSO), 52–53

Student Nonviolent Coordinating Committee (SNCC), 22

Supreme Court, U.S., 25, 68, 105

Swimmer, Ross, 88–90

Thomas, Clarence, 68, 108

Underground Railroad, 74

Unitarian Church, 76–77

United Farm Workers Organizing Committee (UFWOC), 51, 56–59

Vietnam War, 7, 10, 23, 77, 86, 105

Wallace, George, 105

Washington Research Project, 25

Williams, Walter, 36, 37

World War II, 8, 33, 76

Yard, Molly, 67

Young Women's Christian Association (YWCA), 75–76

ABOUT THE AUTHOR

Laurie Lindop has worked as a writer for the Massachusetts Department of Education. She contributed biographies of Gloria Steinem and Toni Morrison to *The Young Reader's Companion to American History*. She lives in Boston, Massachusetts, and is working on her first novel.